LET'S TALK ABOUT

SCIENCE AND RELIGION

OTHER BOOKS IN THE **LET'S TALK ABOUT** SERIES

Let's Talk about Polygamy

Let's Talk about Religion and Mental Health

Let's Talk about the Book of Abraham

Let's Talk about Faith and Intellect

Let's Talk about the Law of Consecration

Let's Talk about Temples and Ritual

Let's Talk about Race and Priesthood

Let's Talk about the Translation of the Book of Mormon

For more information on the other books in the Let's Talk About series, visit DesBook.com/LetsTalk.

LET'S TALK ABOUT

SCIENCE AND RELIGION

JAMIE L. JENSEN
SETH M. BYBEE

DESERET
BOOK

SALT LAKE CITY, UTAH

All images provided by the authors.

Visit us at deseretbook.com

Library of Congress Cataloging-in-Publication Data

CIP on file
ISBN 978-1-63993-149-1

Printed in the United States of America
PubLitho, Draper, UT

10 9 8 7 6 5 4 3 2 1

"All truth is part of the gospel of Jesus Christ. Whether truth comes from a scientific laboratory or by revelation from the Lord, it is compatible."

—President Russell M. Nelson

CONTENTS

CONTENTS

ACKNOWLEDGMENTS

We are incredibly grateful for the many individuals who reviewed this manuscript and offered valuable feedback on tone and content. These include many family and friends and work family in the Department of Biology at Brigham Young University as well as the following specific individuals: Josh Barron, Howard and Jana Bybee, Libby Bybee, Angie Chamberlaine, Megan Childs, Toby Christensen, Stephanie Fleming, Mike Goates, George Handley, Jared Haslam, Jerry and Wendy Haslam, Bruce and Susan Haslam, Spencer Ingley, Rahn Jensen, and Connie Slaughter. Additionally, we owe a great deal of gratitude to Lisa Roper and Kristen Evans for their patience, persistence, and expertise in editing that facilitated creating the balance of religion and science and that kept us *almost* within our word count.

INTRODUCTION

Imagine, as a parent, how you would feel sending your new high school graduate off to college to pursue their dreams. (Maybe you've already experienced this.) You're excited for your child's new adventure, you hope you have prepared them with a strong and unshakeable testimony, but you also worry that they may not have a solid-enough foundation in the gospel to hold to the iron rod in the face of the challenging ideas they will encounter. You pray for them every day and hang on to the hope that the Lord will care for and protect them. Then, one day, your independent "adult" calls you to talk about the latest concept taught in their biology class (perhaps evolution, vaccines, reproductive technologies, or climate change), and they have questions. Are you prepared to have this conversation? Or did your heart just skip a beat because you feel unprepared to discuss these ideas, still unsure yourself about how to reconcile the questions surrounding them?

As educators, we have watched thousands of students navigate new, and often challenging, topics in biology. Most of the time, our students come out of our classes more in awe of their God and more enthusiastic about pursuing His scientific works on earth. Other students, however, allow science to gradually chip away at their faith and replace God's wonder with godlessness. As researchers, we have collected data on the reactions of our students. We've come to understand the different patterns of thinking that occur in a single class; and we've discovered how to teach our students science while protecting them from potentially losing their faith.

Sometimes our role as faithful scientists feels divinely guided. We often pray for personal revelation from the Lord on how to simultaneously teach and inspire our students. However, our reach is limited to the number of students enrolled in our classes each semester. What if all religious individuals were comfortable and confident in exploring scientific discoveries without concern that their testimonies might be shaken? Perhaps it would reverse the concerning trends we see among the youth today. One in four young adults (under age thirty) are unaffiliated with religion.[1] Among teens, this number jumps to one in three and only 40% believe in God with absolute certainty (compared to 63% of their parents).[2]

Our main objective in this book is to equip readers with the thinking patterns and the scientific knowledge necessary to participate in the complex conversations that occur at the intersection of science and religion. We hope to imbue readers with the confidence that science and religion can and do go hand in hand in revealing truth. An important tenet of our religion is to seek truth. Joseph Smith said, "The first and fundamental principle of our holy religion is, that we believe that we have a right to embrace all, and every item of truth, without limitation or without being circumscribed or prohibited by the creeds or superstitious notions of men, or by the dominations of one another, when that truth is clearly demonstrated to our minds, and we have the highest degree of evidence of the same."[3]

As we take a deep dive into science in the pages that follow, we will repeatedly offer potential options for reconciling science with religion and explore how we can use both of these beautiful ways of knowing to bless ourselves, our families, and humanity. In part 1, we explore points that are key to successfully reconciling science and religion. In part 2, we cover what we see as potentially "sticky" topics in the life sciences—topics that are often controversial or sometimes seem at odds with religious teachings—and attempt to understand them in light of both scientific knowledge *and* our religious beliefs. This section does not provide an exhaustive list of the topics you might face yourself or in conversations with neighbors and loved ones, but it is our hope that these examples will help you develop the tools and the perspective necessary to successfully navigate any issue that arises at the intersection of science and religion. So, let's talk about it.

SECTION I

RECONCILING SCIENCE AND RELIGION

CHAPTER 1

THE NATURE AND LIMITATIONS OF SCIENCE AS A WAY OF KNOWING

To successfully reconcile science and religion, it is important to understand the nature and limitations of science as a way of knowing. The purpose of this chapter is to set a foundation of what science is and how it works. We will cover the following:

- The process of hypothesis testing and theory formation
- The difference between hypotheses and theories and the difference between the common use of these terms and their scientific use
- How science as a method of knowing compares to the process of seeking religious truths
- What the limitations of science are and how understanding these limits helps us view science and religion as compatible ways of knowing
- How uncertainty is handled in science through statistics and how we can evaluate sources of information

All this information will lead us to a better understanding of how science is conducted and how it can be complementary with religion as we seek truth. (Also, keep in mind that this is only an introduction to this topic. Many brilliant writers have written entire books on this subject that you can read if you want to dive into this topic in more detail.[1])

The Nature of Science

Let's begin with the nature of science. In other words, how is science done? We'll start with a simple example. Imagine a contraption built out of Lego bricks—some large bricks, some small ones, some little button pieces and grate pieces, and a figurine head stuck to the bottom. This contraption is placed inside an opaque bag with a drawstring at the top. Pretend that you are handed this bag along with a bucket of Legos that contains all the pieces necessary to build a replica of the structure in the bag along with every other piece that Lego makes. Your task is to build a replica of the contraption with one rule: you *cannot* look in the bag. You can only reach your hand in and feel.

Figure 1.1. Lego Contraptions

We have given this task to many students over the years, and they have built a variety of structures, four of which are shown in figure 1.1. The first thing you likely notice is that the colors are all different. Do you notice any structural differences? You can see that two have a button piece on top, while one has a plate and one has a flower piece. Notice that three have a head piece while one used a cylinder. Given time to collaborate with one another and to reach back in the bag to gather further evidence, students usually come to a unanimous consensus on the *structure* of the contraption (that is, all Lego piece types in their replicas are identical). Color, however, remains unresolved . . . for now.

Let's compare this to how science works. First, the purpose of science is to discover truth about the natural world (the contraption in the bag represents truth). But these truths are not always immediately apparent or easily discoverable (it is as though they are in an opaque bag; for example, we can't go back in time to see the process of Creation, we can't shrink down small enough to see the inner workings of a cell nucleus, and so on). Through a process of repeated *hypothesis* testing (is it a head or a cylinder piece?), involving gathering physical data (feeling in the bag), peer collaboration and peer review (comparing your model to others and reviewing the evidence you gathered), and revision (amending your model based on additional data or peer feedback), we come to a *theory* (our overall model of how all the pieces fit together).

Let us define the scientific usage of that term: a theory is the *best* representation of the truth that scientists can build using the *best* available evidence that has been repeatedly tested and confirmed.[2] A theory is different from a "hunch" or a "guess," and misunderstanding this distinction can sometimes be a stumbling block for people. They may assume that if a scientist calls something a *theory*, it means the idea is very tentative and therefore, perhaps, not to be trusted. Instead, when scientists arrive at a theory, we can feel comfortable that they have done their very best to test and explain a natural phenomenon.

Let's return to the question of color. In our scenario, the color of the blocks could not be resolved given the limitations of the activity (you cannot look in the bag). However, we once had a student ask if they could put their cell phone in the bag and take a picture! Brilliant! New technologies, or the unearthing of new evidence, often lead us closer and closer to the truth. But, like color, there are always unknown aspects of our theories. This does not mean the theory is arbitrary or tentative; far from it. Theories are well-established frameworks through which we view the world. But parts of theories can be amended or refined. Knowing this can help us feel more comfortable when religious truths and scientific theories seem like they might be in conflict. We need to delay judgment until we can (and in some cases we may never in this lifetime) resolve some of these unknowns.

The Nature of Religion

Let's compare this process of finding scientific truths to the process of finding religious truths. Surprisingly, it is not that much different, though there are some key contrasts. Let's start with the invitation found in Moroni 10:3–5. It is a simple and elegant example of the nature of religious inquiry. Moroni is concluding the record that he and his father, Mormon, have compiled. He then turns to the reader and proposes an experiment:

> Behold, I would exhort you that when ye shall read these things, if it be wisdom in God that ye should read them, that ye would remember how merciful the Lord hath been unto the children of men, from the creation of Adam even down until the time that ye shall receive these things, . . . I would exhort you that ye would ask God, the Eternal Father, in the name of Christ, if these things are not true; and if ye shall ask with a sincere heart, with real intent, having faith in Christ, he will manifest the truth of it unto you, by the power of the Holy Ghost. And by the power of the Holy Ghost ye may know the truth of all things. (Moroni 10:3–5)

Similar to the scientific process, we are presented with a hypothesis to test: the record is true (with the alternative being that the record is *not* true). To test this hypothesis, we can ask God. This is similar to performing an experiment to gather data. Moroni also gives us our predicted results: if this record is true (my proposed hypothesis), and I ask God (that is, I pray about it), then I will be given confirmation by the Holy Ghost. In other words, the data we are collecting are manifestations from the Holy Ghost. If we receive a manifestation and we know how to interpret it, then we will know that the record is true. If we don't, then we won't know. Perhaps we have not yet learned to listen to the Holy Ghost; perhaps we are not sincere in our asking; or perhaps God has other reasons for delaying an answer.

Now here is where this process differs from science. In

science, we gather physical data from the natural world using instrumentation (like scales, rulers, survey instruments, calipers, thermometers, and spectrometers). In religion, we gather data that is beyond the natural world (like inspired understanding, feelings, and revelations from the Holy Ghost). Our data comes from the spiritual world through spiritual instrumentation (like faith, prayer, listening, and priesthood blessings). But in both cases, we need to be trained on how to use the instrumentation to recognize and interpret the data. And in both cases, the data are available to anyone who wants to learn to interpret it.

In the case of religion, however, these points of data are shareable but not transferable. If I run an experiment to measure the effects of exercise on body mass index, I can measure the amount of exercise and the subsequent body mass indices of my research participants, and I can then show these data to you. If we are both trained appropriately, we will both come to the same conclusion. But in testing the truthfulness of the Book of Mormon, I can measure the feelings I have and the spiritual confirmation I receive; I can share these spiritual data with others in the form of my testimony, but I cannot transfer my faith or confirmation to them. Each individual person must gather the data for themselves. This spiritual process of inquiry is no less legitimate and no less critical to our understanding of the world than scientific experimentation. The evidence just takes a different form. And each way of knowing answers different questions.

The Limitations of Science

It's important to understand the limitations of science in answering questions about the world. The first limitation is that we can *never* prove anything beyond *reasonable* doubt. This is because of two key facts: (1) scientific theories are built with certain assumptions, and (2) there is always the possibility that an alternative explanation will arise later that can better explain the same phenomena.

First, let's deal with assumptions. An *assumption* is

"something we accept as true without proof."[3] In science, we make a few fundamental assumptions that are necessary for the process of science to work.[4] First, we assume that everything that occurs in our universe has a natural cause or explanation. Science does not rely on supernatural explanations. This does not mean that a supernatural force, such as God, cannot be involved; it just means science needs a reasonable, natural cause to study. If there is a phenomenon here on earth that cannot be explained through natural causes and can be attributed to God only, then according to science, the explanation would be incorrect (we will visit this topic more in chapter 3).

Second, we assume that we can learn about these natural causes by gathering evidence from the natural world. In other words, we assume that these causes are knowable, that they are not hidden or impossible to comprehend. Now, this assumption may seem to contradict a scripture that we, as Latter-day Saints, hold dear: "Behold, great and marvelous are the works of the Lord. How unsearchable are the depths of the mysteries of him; and it is impossible that man should find out all his ways" (Jacob 4:8). However, we believe that this scientific assumption refers only to the current workings of the *natural* world. Any mysteries of God that are beyond the natural world cannot be understood through science.

Third, we assume that these natural causes operate in a consistent way—that gravity, for example, works on a ball in North Dakota the same way it works on a stick in Tennessee, or that isotopes, like carbon-14, decay today in the same way they decayed a thousand years ago. This is probably one of the most contested assumptions in science, and as a consequence, it is also the one to which scientists are most attuned; we test and retest our experiments under a variety of circumstances. At this point, we are unaware that this assumption has ever been disproven. But that does not mean it cannot be falsified in the future. These three assumptions are why scientists never claim to know the ultimate truth.

The second key limitation is that there is always the

possibility that an alternative explanation will arise that can explain the same phenomena. To illustrate, we'll share a brief example. Since the discovery of fire, humans have been making observations about its behavior. When you burn a piece of wood, smoke rises into the air and the remaining ash weighs less than the original piece of wood. In the late 1600s to early 1800s, chemists began to formulate an explanation for this phenomenon: combustible material is composed of "earth" plus "phlogiston" (pronounced flō-ˈjis-tən). When burned, the phlogiston rises and the earth remains as ash. This explanation perfectly explained why ashes weigh less than wood and why the smoke rises.[5] However, a chemist named Levoisier[6] began burning other substances and found that magnesium gains weight when burned. This eventually led to the discovery of oxygen and the chemical process of combustion that transforms organic compounds in wood into carbon dioxide gas and water, and combines with magnesium to create a heavier magnesium oxide. We then had a new, better explanation for the same phenomenon (the burning of wood) that *also* explained other things, like the burning of magnesium.

This is the beautiful process of science. As we discover more, our explanations are refined (and sometimes, though rarely, completely overturned). This is another reason why scientists never completely "prove" anything. Knowing this can make us feel more comfortable when something we "know" now in science seems to contradict something we "know" now in religion. Be patient—science (and religion, for that matter) is a progressive process. And we know that "truth does not conflict with truth, but . . . all truth may be circumscribed into one great whole."[7]

Statistical Reasoning

So how can we conclude anything if there is always uncertainty? This is where statistics come in. It is not a question of whether we are certain or uncertain. It is more a question of *how* certain we are and *how much* certainty we are willing to accept. For example, if we flip a coin 100 times, it will most likely land on heads somewhere around 50 times and on tails 50 times. It is theoretically possible, although extremely unlikely, to flip 90 heads and only 10 tails. Obviously, the further from a 50/50 ratio we get, the more we start to suspect that something is up with that coin. As a rule of thumb, scientists generally say that if something happens less than 5% of the time by chance, there is probably something fishy going on. In other words, if I get a flip of 98 heads and 2 tails (something that happens way less than 5% of the time by chance, even though it *can* happen by chance), I'm going to determine that the coin is probably not fair.

So we must decide how much uncertainty we are willing to accept, knowing that there will always be a small chance that we are wrong. Of course, our willingness to accept uncertainty changes depending on the consequences. For example, when testing a cancer treatment drug, we might decide to only accept a 0.001%, rather than 5%, chance that we are wrong (that is, we want to be extremely sure that our treatment is more effective than an alternate treatment).

To summarize, we can't eliminate all uncertainty; that is the nature of science. But we can have a great deal of confidence in our findings by using statistical reasoning. This same uncertainty is true in our religious faith. We don't think anyone would declare that they have a sure knowledge of all things spiritual. Otherwise, what would be the point of faith? We have faith in a lot of things, and that is okay. This is how we learn and progress.

Alma compared the word of God to a seed and encouraged us to conduct an experiment by exercising faith (see Alma 32:27–28). Once we've planted the seed and seen the good results, he asks, "And now, behold, is your knowledge perfect?" He answers, "Yea, your knowledge is perfect *in that thing*, and your faith is dormant; and this because you know" (v. 34; emphasis added). However, he cautions, "Behold, after ye have tasted this light is your knowledge perfect? Behold I say unto you, Nay; neither must ye lay aside your faith, for ye have only exercised your faith to plant the seed that ye might try the experiment to know if the seed was good" (vv. 35–36). In other words, you have a perfect (or near perfect) knowledge of only this *one thing*. This doesn't mean that you've eliminated all uncertainty or that you should stop inquiring or testing your faith and gathering more evidence. Alma invites us, "Let us nourish it [the tree that has sprouted] with great care, that it may get root, that it may grow up, and bring forth fruit unto us" (v. 37).

And he promises, "If ye will . . . nourish the tree as it beginneth to grow, by your faith with great diligence . . . it shall take root; and behold it shall be a tree springing up unto everlasting life" (v. 41). The Lord offers us, again and again, the opportunity to use this spiritual process of inquiry to gain a deeper understanding of His plan of salvation. Repeatedly He asks us to "prove me now herewith" (Malachi 3:10), to see for ourselves, to gather our own data, and to confirm through faithful investigation that what He says is true, and that will lead to "peace in this world and eternal life in the world to come" (Doctrine and Covenants 59:23).

Evaluating Sources

Understanding the limitations of science, how do we know which scientific sources to trust? To explain this, we'll briefly outline a well-cited and oft-used framework called the "CRAAP Test."[8] The *C* stands for *currency*. More current information is generally more trustworthy. For example, scientific texts from the 1800s supporting bloodletting to cure disease would never be consulted today. As science discovers more truth, our understanding changes, and some sources that were considered appropriate at the time they were written are no longer appropriate today. This also applies to religious sources. If we want to know God's law for us today, we would consult the new law established by Jesus Christ in Matthew 5:38–48 rather than the laws established in the time of Moses with the children of Israel in Exodus 21–23 (an "eye for an eye" and a "tooth for a tooth").

The *R* stands for *relevance.* Consider first whether the source was intended to answer your question and second if you are the intended audience. For example, if I am looking for information about the effectiveness of a given drug, the scientific article describing the clinical trials that led to its approval by the FDA may be packed with scientific jargon and other details that make it hard for me to fully understand. What I really need is an entry from Mayoclinic.org that summarizes the relevant information in a way that is accessible to a more generalized audience. The principle of relevance can also be applied to the scriptures and other religious writings. For example, while the Word of Wisdom (see Doctrine and Covenants 89) is true scripture and contains valuable insights on good health, you would not consult it for questions about how much tithing to pay.

The first *A* stands for *authority.* Does the person who wrote the source have the correct credentials to be considered an authority? For example, if you are looking for answers about the effect of pesticides on insect pollinator populations, you would hopefully consult a biologist over a Hollywood actor. The same rule can be applied to religious sources: if you are looking for directions that apply to the Church as a whole, you would look to the prophet, not to some random person sharing an opinion on the internet.

The second *A* stands for *accuracy.* To determine how accurate a scientific source is, it's a good idea to ask *where* it is published. Scientific journals have strict processes in place to try to avoid publishing misinformation. We are not saying these processes are foolproof; occasionally garbage gets through. But faulty publications are usually quickly retracted when other experts in the field see it and alert the journal. One process is called *peer review.* We can apply this concept to our scripture study as well. As Latter-day Saints, we are blessed to have the Joseph Smith Translation that corrects many of the accuracy errors in the Bible, and we have the Book of Mormon to further clarify doctrine.

Finally, the *P* stands for *purpose*. Is the source meant to inform you? Persuade you? Drive an agenda? You can usually figure out a source's purpose by looking at the media through which it is published and discovering if the source has a vested interest in the information. In applying *purpose* to religious writings, we know that the Lord has given us the gospel and the scriptures to fulfil His work and glory—"to bring to pass the immortality and eternal life of man" (Moses 1:39). We can seek religious sources that promote faith and bring us closer to this goal rather than dabbling in unfriendly sources aimed at undermining our faith.

Conclusion

Understanding how science is done and its limitations as a method of knowing can help us better integrate it with the knowledge we gain from spiritual pursuits. Truth exists, and God wants us to pursue truth through the many means He has made available. We can learn about the natural world through science, and we can learn about our relationship to God, the plan of salvation, and how to obtain eternal life through religion. If understood correctly, truth will not conflict with truth, and both will lead to a perfect whole.

CHAPTER 2

SCIENCE IS AGNOSTIC

Agnostic means "without belief," specifically without belief in God. When we say that "science is agnostic," we mean that science cannot prove there *is* a God any more than it can prove that there *is not.* This is something that is often misunderstood, both by scientists and nonscientists alike.[1] To better understand this idea, we will discuss the following:

- The types of questions science can and cannot answer
- The difference between scientific data with appropriate conclusions and value-based judgments based on those data
- The differences between atheism, agnosticism, and theism and how science is agnostic
- Spiritual knowledge as an equally valid way of understanding the world

By understanding that science is constrained to the natural, physical world and does not attempt to gather data about spiritual things, we avoid setting up the false idea that science and religion are mutually exclusive. We will start with an illustration.

Cloning a Mammoth

Using the DNA from multiple mammoth remains, scientists have been able to piece together most of the DNA needed to reconstruct a mammoth.[2] This has led to the real possibility that woolly mammoths could be brought back from extinction. Using the same procedure that allowed for the cloning of Dolly the sheep,[3] scientists can place the mammoth DNA into the fertilized egg of an Asian elephant (the closest living relative to the mammoth).[4] However, because the DNA is not complete (we just have pieces) scientists are proposing to combine what mammoth DNA we have with the DNA of an Asian elephant[5] to *make* a mammoth.[6] Either way, the endpoint is the birth of a woolly mammoth to an Asian elephant mother.

Let's say that the president of a biotech company approaches you about being an investor in their cause to resurrect the mammoth species. Pause for a moment and think about the questions you would ask before investing. What do you want to know? The first question often thrown out is, "Have you seen *Jurassic Park*?" While meant as a joke, it does bring up many important questions: Would recreating mammoths be dangerous to humans? Is it even possible? What is the probability of success? Would the creature really be a mammoth? Would the mammoth be able to survive in the current environments available on earth? What impact will the mammoth have on modern ecosystems? Is it safe for the mother Asian elephant? They are endangered, after all.[7] And, of course, this question: Is it ethical to bring back a species that went extinct on its own?

The first set of questions posed are answerable by science. Scientists know a lot about woolly mammoths including how large they were and potentially how dangerous, what they ate, with what other species they competed, what temperatures they can tolerate, and more.[8] Scientists have also already successfully developed the techniques needed to perform the procedure,[9] so they know a bit about safety and the probability of success. However, the question "Is it ethical?" is not answerable by science. Going back to one of the fundamental assumptions of science—that everything has a natural cause or explanation—we know that science, as a field, is only able to answer questions about the physical world or about physical phenomena. A question about ethics cannot be answered with a physical explanation. We need a different "way of knowing" to answer this question—a way that involves ethics, morals, and even religious belief.

Scientific Decisions versus Value Judgments

As this scenario illustrates, there are clear limitations to what science can contribute. We sometimes see, however, people entangling value statements with scientific statements, without distinguishing between them. For example, regarding climate change, science can tell you that the earth has warmed, why the earth has warmed, what solutions are likely to reverse climate change, and even what consequences will result if current practices contributing to climate change continue. However, science *cannot* tell you what you are *morally* obligated to do. That being said, scientists often *do* offer an opinion (a value statement) about the issues they study. There's nothing wrong with that; but the value statement is often communicated incorrectly, and values rather than data often have a greater influence on people's responses to science.[10]

So, for example, climate scientists may deeply understand the data (or even gather the data themselves) and conclude that the earth is in great danger. Then, they may conclude, based on their own values and morals, that everyone should feel obligated to change their behavior in dramatic ways (for example, not having any children, eating only plant-based products, or eliminating all use of fossil fuels). Notice where the science ended and the value judgment began: the *science* demonstrated that the problem is severe, but their *values* told them that people should put the environment above basic human instincts or economic issues.

Understanding the difference between science and values is important for scientists and educators who communicate data, as well as for students, nonscientists, policymakers, and others who receive and interpret the communication. By understanding this difference, we can listen to scientists and disentangle the data (that we can all analyze with a critical eye) from the values (with which we may or may not agree). In the context of climate change, this means we can see the data that show a steady increase in global temperatures corresponding with the release of carbon dioxide into the atmosphere from the burning of fossil fuels[11] and conclude that the climate is changing and humans are contributing. But we can disagree with how we prioritize solutions (for instance, some might prefer nuclear power to solar and wind, and others might believe that economic consequences should be weighted heavier than the benefits of eliminating fossil fuels).

Let's explore further what we mean by "value judgments" or "ethics." Both rely on understanding that is *not* gained through the scientific method. Instead, values are individual beliefs that are a result of our upbringing, our culture, our worldviews, and our experiences.[12] These values can be sacred and influenced by our religious beliefs (for example, as Latter-day Saints, we place great value on family).[13] Our ethical understanding—that is, our understanding of what is morally right and wrong—is based on our values; but because values differ between individuals, our ethical understanding may also differ (what one person believes is morally wrong may not be interpreted as wrong by another). An understanding of science may help us better weigh our values when making ethical decisions, but it cannot pronounce a "right" or a "wrong" because science does not deal with religious or spiritual beliefs—it is *agnostic*, without belief.

Atheism, Agnosticism, and Theism

Because science is limited to natural or physical explanations and cannot answer questions about the divine, it cannot offer evidence *for* or *against* the existence of God. We will illustrate this with a scenario. Over the centuries, human civilizations have offered many different views on how modern-day diversity came to be on our planet.[14] A handful of them are listed in table 1.

Table 1. A Spectrum of Views about the Development of Modern-Day Diversity

Model	Brief Description
Young Earth Creationism	The Creation took place in six twenty-four-hour periods less than ten thousand years ago by God as literally interpreted from Genesis.
Day-Age Creationism	The Creation took place in six periods of unknown length, but as described in Genesis.
Progressive Creationism	There were multiple God-guided Creation events that happened over hundreds of millions of years.
Theistic Evolution	Modern diversity arose through evolution, with God guiding it.
Agnostic Evolution	Modern diversity arose through evolution, with no statement on whether or not God was involved.
Atheistic Evolution	Modern diversity arose through evolution, and God was *not* involved.

For now, don't consider which model you currently accept (these models will be discussed further in chapter 7). Rather, consider which of these is compatible with the scientific evidence of evolution. Young Earth creationism is not supported by the science that shows our earth has existed for at least 4.5 billion years[15] and that life has existed upwards of 3.5 billion years.[16] Day-age and progressive creationism are difficult to fit within the bounds of the scientific evidence, but they could, depending on how strictly one adheres to the details found in Genesis. (For example, in day-age creationism, does the order of Creation laid out in Genesis have to be exact, meaning that plants were created before the sun [see Genesis 1:11–14])? And in progressive creationism, does the divine override natural processes or simply guide them?) Thus, we will not make a judgment call on those two for now. From a scientific standpoint, however, we can clearly accept theistic, agnostic, and atheistic viewpoints since they conclude that evolution occurred according to the available scientific evidence.

Our next question is, which of these last three models makes a statement for which we have no *scientific* evidence? That's right—*both* theistic and atheistic models go a step beyond the science: although science says evolution occurred, it is our *belief* that says that God does or does not exist. Atheism is just as much a belief system as theism. Thus, the most appropriate version of evolution, from a scientific standpoint, is agnostic, often referred to as "naturalistic" evolution. Let us again emphasize that *science is agnostic*—without belief. It is quite common for people to misunderstand this principle, believing that to accept evolution you must be an atheist; in a recent study half of all undergraduates reported this belief.[17]

The Importance of Spiritual Knowledge

Does this mean that the religious beliefs that inform our value judgments are not important? Of course not! They are simply a different way of knowing. And, for those of us who are Latter-day Saints, they are an important way of knowing. We have been taught to "seek . . . out of the best books words of wisdom" and to "seek learning, even by study and also by faith" (Doctrine and Covenants 88:118) and that "to be learned is good if [we] hearken unto the counsels of God" (2 Nephi 9:29). President Spencer W. Kimball said that "preeminent among all activities in this life is preparing [ourselves] for eternal life by subjugating the flesh, subjecting the body to the spirit, overcoming weakness, and so governing [ourselves] that [we] may give leadership to others. Important, but of second priority, comes the knowledge associated with life in mortality."[18] In other words, spiritual understanding should come first. President Kimball continued, "As we master ourselves, we will learn to master the earth and its elements."[19]

As Latter-day Saints, we value learning through both religion and science because doing so allows us to discover a fuller version of the truth. President Dallin H. Oaks wisely counseled that "'scientific truth' is not the whole of life. Those who do not learn 'by study and also by faith' (Doctrine and Covenants 88:118) limit their understanding of truth to what they can verify by scientific means. That puts artificial limits on their pursuit of truth."[20] We are counseled to learn "of things both in heaven and in the earth, and under the earth; things which have been, things which are, things which must shortly come to pass; things which are at home, things which are abroad; the wars and the perplexities of the nations, and the judgments which are on the land; and a knowledge also of countries and of kingdoms" that you "may be prepared in all things when [God] shall send you again to magnify the calling whereunto [He has] called you, and the mission with which [He has] commissioned you" (Doctrine and Covenants 88:79–80). As Latter-day Saints who have the privilege of having access to both secular knowledge and spiritual knowledge, we can be a light to those around us and even to the nations by seeking knowledge through both avenues.

Conclusion

By understanding that science is agnostic, we can avoid viewing it as a threat to our faith. As we seek scientific understanding, we are bound to encounter many different experts with a variety of values. These variations in values will inevitably lead to different interpretations of scientific understanding. For example, science can tell you what materials to use to create great paintings, but it can't tell you what is beautiful. Science can tell you how much of the body is still functioning after a tragic accident or at end-of-life, but it can't tell you the decisions you should make about preserving life. Science can tell you which deterrents are more successful at curbing crime, but it can't tell you whether corporal punishment is ethical or not. And the list goes on and on. Being able to differentiate between the scientific data and the value-based interpretations and implementation of that data allows for productive dialogue about scientific issues in which differing opinions are valued and even fostered to create a better world. A diversity of thought is not a bad thing; it often leads to superior solutions to societal problems.

CHAPTER 3

BASE YOUR FAITH IN GOD ON CORRECT EVIDENCE

Let's continue to distinguish our two ways of knowing, science and religion, by discussing faith and how we come to a knowledge of God. We will emphasize the importance of *basing your faith in God on the correct evidence.* Let's recap some important principles we learned in chapter 1 about the nature of religion:

1. Religion aims to find truth about things beyond the natural world.
2. Religion follows a similar pattern of hypothesis testing as science.
3. In comparison to scientific evidence, religious evidence is interpreted using different, spiritual tools, and as such, it is shareable but not transferrable to another person.

Is this to say that religion cannot be a source of knowledge about *natural* things? Not exactly. We have many examples of religious knowledge that directly *apply* to the physical world (the Word of Wisdom [see Doctrine and Covenants 89], the law of chastity, and our stewardship responsibilities over our earthly blessings[1]). However, these revelations about physical aspects of our lives are part of our spiritual relationship with our Heavenly Father; some are part of our covenants, and they are about being obedient to His commandments. That is to say, even though these truths relate to physical things, they are part of our spiritual understanding. We would like to highlight three important points in this chapter:

- If we place our faith in God primarily on His explaining

gaps in our current scientific understanding (that is, if we believe in a "God of the Gaps"), we have inadvertently allowed the possibility that science will destroy our testimony.

- Seeking for physical signs of God's existence, while possible to receive, equally puts our testimony in jeopardy.
- Basing our testimony on spiritual evidence is the surest way to strengthen it and protect it from the doubt that can come from the misinterpretations of earthly knowledge and experience.

A God of the Gaps

A faulty pattern of reasoning common among religious individuals is a mentality that builds a spiritual foundation on a "God of the Gaps." Three thousand years before Christ, in the Bronze Age, the Greek Gods of Olympus played a large role in people's lives.[2] They were deemed responsible for many scientific phenomena that, at the time, could not be otherwise explained. For example, Zeus was the god of lightning, Poseidon was the god of hurricanes and earthquakes, and Demeter was the goddess of the harvest. So, if lightning struck your ox, or an earthquake destroyed your city, or your crops failed, the event was blamed on the wrath of the gods. The ancient Greeks used the gods to explain phenomena that they did not understand (the "gaps"). Not surprisingly, when scientific exploration and experimentation led to *scientific* explanations for these gaps—lightning is an electrical discharge between clouds and the ground;[3] earthquakes result from shifting tectonic plates;[4] and crops fail for any number of reasons, from drought to infestation[5]—their belief in their gods began to diminish.[6]

Let us give another biological example. Modern-day whales have been swimming in our oceans for the last 50 million years.[7] By the 1800s, it was well known that whales breathed air with lungs, gave birth to live young, and fed those young with milk—just like other land-dwelling mammals. It was a mystery, however, as to how whales, who are presumably mammals like cows, horses, dogs, cats, and humans, ended up living in the sea. Additionally, all other mammals have four limbs, but whales have only two, even though their embryos have four.[8] Whales have muscles similar to other land-dwelling mammals, so their swimming motion is up and down, in comparison to the side-to-side motion of all other fish (for example, trout and sharks).[9] The "God of the Gaps" explanation for whales was simply that God created them in their present form and placed them in the sea (Genesis 1:21).

Fossil evidence discovered in the late 1900s, however, revealed ancient creatures that appear to be intermediate forms between a four-legged, land-dwelling mammal and the two-legged, sea-dwelling mammal whales of today. An ancestor of whales from 50 million years ago had teeth to hunt fish and other features adapted for life in the water, but its ears were not yet adapted for aquatic hearing or deep diving.[10] Later fossils from 48 million years ago showed the animal's ears had adapted for an aquatic environment.[11] And fossils from 46 million years ago show a powerful swimming tail (one that moved up and down), reduced hind limbs that would have been inefficient on land, nostrils that had moved back on the snout toward the top of the head, and ears highly adapted to aquatic life.[12] By 36 million years ago, we can see nostrils that had fused into a single blowhole toward the top of the head and hind limbs that would have been completely incapable of supporting the animal on land, confirming that these animals had become entirely aquatic.[13, 14]

Additionally, all these creatures share the unique bone structures of the ankle and inner ear of modern-day whales.[15] Using modern molecular techniques, scientists have compared the DNA of modern whales with other mammals and found that hippos are their closest living relatives.[16] In addition, modern whales have all the bones of a human hand in their flippers[17] and even leftover pelvic bones.[18] Thus, the evidence suggested to scientists that modern whales descended from a land-dwelling, four-legged mammal and evolved into their current two-limbed aquatic form. Gap closed. With this new scientific understanding came a danger for those who had based their faith in God on the unexplainable appearance of modern whales in the ocean at the beginning of time; for these individuals, the newly discovered scientific evidence might shake that faith. And sometimes, tragically, to avoid losing their faith, instead of being patient and waiting for further understanding, some individuals may pretend these data do not exist or try to explain them away with alternate, nonscientific scenarios or even conspiracy theories.

Let's look at one last, more recent example: human morality. Why do humans have an innate sense of right and wrong? Why do we feel disgust toward injustice? Why did the American forefathers write that the unalienable rights of people were "life, liberty, and the pursuit of happiness"?[19] Why do humans seem to have the inborn moral values of fairness, care for others, respect for authority, and loyalty to one's group?[20] Why does research show that nearly from birth, we have a sense of fairness and a desire to act with compassion toward others?[21] Some would argue that this built-in sense of morality is endowed in us by God, that there is no physical or biological explanation, and therefore, it must be only due to God's handiwork. However, evolutionary biologists and anthropologists would argue that the behavior is simply embedded in our genetics, the result of evolution through natural selection—those who possessed these moral tendencies were more welcomed into the group and therefore more likely to breed and pass on those "moral" genes—and scientists have evidence that supports this hypothesis.[22] In fact, many nonhuman species display similar moral and cooperative behaviors.[23]

So if morality is (1) not exclusive to humans and (2) evolutionarily beneficial and therefore likely to have evolved, does this mean that God is not real? Of course not. We readily acknowledge that morality is part of our identity as children of God and that it is a gift (see Doctrine and Covenants 101:78).

It is a necessary trait that our mortal tabernacles must possess to exercise our agency and participate in the plan of salvation. But perhaps God used natural processes to produce this morality. However, if our testimonies are based on the idea that morality cannot be explained *except* by the presence of God, our testimonies may be put at risk. The key in both of these scenarios is not to fill gaps in scientific understanding with an exclusively divine explanation because those gaps have the possibility of being filled with a newly discovered and rigorously tested scientific explanation.

Seeking for Signs

All of these scenarios are examples of basing one's testimony on a "God of the Gaps"—that is, inserting God as an explanation for anything that science cannot currently explain. A similar pattern of thinking is to try to use science and natural phenomena to prove God's existence—for example, by replacing actual scientific evidence with fake scientific explanations that favor supernatural causes for physical phenomena (we will talk more on this in chapter 4) or by seeking for physical signs of God's existence.

In Alma 30, we see a classic example of this pattern of reasoning in Korihor, the anti-Christ. He was going about the land trying to convince the Nephites that a person cannot know that God is real because there is no physical evidence (see Alma 30:26). Alma asks him an interesting and profound question: "And now what evidence have ye that there is no God, or that Christ cometh not? I say unto you that ye have none, save it be your word only" (Alma 30:40). Alma is emphasizing a key aspect of the nature of science that we have already discussed: science is agnostic. We do not have scientific evidence *for* or *against* the existence of God. A further response of "Absence of evidence is *not* evidence of absence" would be appropriate. In response, Korihor asserts, "If thou wilt show me a sign, that I may be convinced that there is a God, yea, show unto me that he hath power, and then will I be convinced of the truth of thy words"(Alma 30:43). Korihor is asking for physical, scientific proof of God's existence. But is this how we are to seek a testimony of our Father in Heaven?

The Lord clearly teaches that signs follow our faith, not the other way around: "But, behold, faith cometh not by signs, but signs follow those that believe" (Doctrine and Covenants 63:9). This brings us to an important scripture in Alma 30, verse 44, where Alma proclaims that "all things denote there is a God; yea, even the earth, and all things that are upon the face of it, yea, and its motion, yea, and also all the planets which move in their regular form do witness that there is a Supreme Creator." This implies that physical things, things of the natural world, *can* serve as evidence of God. However, these things are evidence of God to those who have already obtained a testimony of God through *spiritual* evidence. These physical evidences *follow* our faith; they do not *build* our faith. For a nonbeliever, these evidences would hardly witness to them of a Supreme Creator because they would not recognize such evidence until after they have come to know God through spiritual means.

Base Your Testimony on Spiritual Evidence

It is dangerous to believe in God only when His existence resolves uncertainty, when His existence explains things that you do not understand. What happens when science comes up with a reasonable and even testable explanation for a "gap" in our understanding? Does your faith disappear because something you attributed to God can now be explained by science? It won't if your belief is not based in God's filling the gaps.

Or what if your testimony is dependent upon physical, scientific evidence that God exists? What happens if that evidence cannot be found? We need a shift in our mindset such that our belief in God is for an entirely different reason—not because He can explain the gaps in our current understanding or because we have physical proof, but because He gives us spiritual understanding and because we have felt His presence in our lives (spiritual evidence, not scientific evidence). This leads to the very important question "On what *should* we base our testimonies?," to which we firmly respond: "On *spiritual* knowledge."

President Dallin H. Oaks defined a testimony as "a personal witness borne to our souls by the Holy Ghost that certain facts of eternal significance are true and that we know them to be true. Such facts include the nature of the Godhead and our relationship to its three members, the effectiveness of the Atonement, and the reality of the Restoration."[24] Let's break this down: First, a testimony is a personal witness. We learned in chapter 1 about the nature of religious evidence and how each individual may obtain it for themselves. Second, a testimony comes by the Holy Ghost. Indeed, Christ emphasized this to Peter when He said, "Blessed art thou, Simon Barjona: for flesh and blood hath not revealed it unto thee, but my Father which is in heaven" (Matthew 16:17). Scientific evidence will not reveal God to us; God is not in the gaps in our scientific understanding. A knowledge of God comes through the Holy Ghost. Third, a testimony deals with certain facts of eternal significance. In other words, a testimony pertains to spiritual matters. It is a belief in or knowledge of spiritual things. But rest assured, as President Oaks emphasized, "When we know spiritual truths by spiritual means, we can be just as sure of the knowledge as scholars and scientists are of the different kinds of knowledge they have acquired by different methods."[25]

Just like there are steps to obtaining scientific understanding, there are steps to obtaining spiritual knowledge. First, we can develop a firm desire to know the truth. As Alma teaches, if you but "desire to believe" (Alma 32:27), you have already taken the first step to obtaining a testimony. Second, you can strive to obey God's commandments. The Lord taught, "If any man will do his will, he shall know of the doctrine, whether it be of God, or whether I speak of myself" (John 7:16–17). Third, you can put forth the effort to know. Just as we do not gain a knowledge of algebra without cracking a textbook or attending a class, we will not gain spiritual knowledge without seeking for it through study, prayer, church attendance, and so on. We are promised, "Ask, and ye shall receive; knock, and it shall be opened to you" (3 Nephi 27:29).

Lastly, share your testimony. Unlike worldly goods that diminish as you share them, testimonies, in contrast, grow as you share them. President Oaks commented that "some testimonies are better gained on the feet bearing them than on the knees praying for them."[26] By sharing our testimonies with others, we can prompt them to desire a testimony for themselves. As we emphasized, spiritual evidence is shareable but not transferrable. Each of us are required to build a testimony for ourselves. But sharing the correct evidence for our testimonies—explaining the *spiritual* evidence we have gained for why we believe in God and Jesus Christ—can help others who are working to shift the focus of their belief from gaps in scientific understanding to true spiritual understanding.

Conclusion

There are dangers in basing your testimony on a "God of the Gaps," which includes using God as an explanation for things that science can't *currently* explain, attempting to prove God's existence with scientific evidence, and seeking for physical signs of God's existence. All of these lead to a shaky foundation for a testimony, one that can be pushed about by the winds of new scientific discovery. Instead, we should build our testimonies on *spiritual* evidence, which includes revelation and promptings from the Holy Ghost that come after sincere seeking through faith and obedience to the commandments. It would be easy for God to resolve the question of His existence and power. However, in line with Satan's plan (see Moses 4:1–4), this would not provide us with the growth and knowledge required to become like God. Testimonies built on spiritual evidence cannot be refuted by scientific evidence, nor are they influenced or shaken by the latest scientific discoveries. Spiritual truth remains constant.

CHAPTER 4

TEACH TRUE SCIENCE, NOT PSEUDOSCIENCE

The next important point we'll discuss is teaching real science rather than resorting to pseudoscientific explanations. In this chapter, we will do the following:

- Directly confront an example involving vaccines and autism, where pseudoscience has become culturally established as "truth" that has been pushed by both scientists and nonscientists alike
- Provide the most up-to-date scientific data and findings on the issue
- Examine the importance of science from a religious lens
- Emphasize the importance of teaching correct science in our homes, bathed in the light of the gospel

The goal of this chapter is to provide a model for detecting and rooting out pseudoscience from our homes so that we and our children can be confident that we have the best information.

Before we tackle this, Jamie will help illustrate and define pseudoscience with a little anecdote.

> Who knew that a routine eye exam could cause me to lose a semester of school and change the course of my college career? I was a nineteen-year-old sophomore at BYU when I went home for Christmas. While there, I headed to my optometrist to update my contact lens prescription. During the slit lamp exam, the doctor paused and took a deep breath.
>
> "Jamie," he said, "I'm going to call an ophthalmologist.

I want him to examine you right away. You've got pressure and swelling on your optic nerve. It looks like you've got papilledema."

At the time, I'd never even heard of papilledema, but it sounded serious. I couldn't decide whether to be concerned about the stress I could hear in the doctor's voice or irritated that I'd be missing a New Year's Eve party. After visiting the ophthalmologist, concern won out. The ophthalmologist, too, saw papilledema and explained to me that this meant my optic nerve was bowed out, indicating swelling in my brain, possibly caused by a brain bleed, tumor, or spinal meningitis.

I was rushed to another location for a spinal tap, my mom with me every step of the way. We tried to talk and reassure each other. However, as the day wore on, my situation became more dire, especially the moment when, twenty-four hours after getting a spinal tap, I experienced a severe complication that caused cerebrospinal fluid to leak from the puncture and my brain to no longer be floating nicely in the liquid inside my skull. The excruciating headache that followed (and fear I wasn't going to make it through the night) landed me in the hospital for an emergency blood patch.

It was shortly after my hospital stay, after seeing several more specialists, that they finally concluded what I had was called "pseudo-papilledema," or "fake-papilledema," caused by another rare condition called optic nerve drusen. (Optic nerve drusen really boils down to "optic nerve boogers" that cause the nerve to buckle a little and appear to have swelling behind it.) It's a rather harmless condition. Unfortunately, this fiasco ended up delaying my return to BYU and my subsequent withdrawal for a semester to recover.

Pseudoscience Causes Physical Harm

We tell you this anecdote to illustrate a very important principle: when pseudoscience masquerades as real science, the unintended consequences can be catastrophic. In this anecdote, pseudo-papilledema was masquerading as a severe and potentially life-threatening disease. And unnecessary suffering resulted based on the interpretations of "false data" that seemed to be very real. Just like pseudo-papilledema is *not* papilledema, pseudoscience is *not* science—it is "fake science" that can mislead people. The consequences of pseudoscience can be severe, and those who adopt it as truth are often innocent victims.

There are several examples from the history of science where pseudoscience, masquerading as real science, has caused great physical harm. The first involves the measles, mumps, and rubella vaccine (the MMR). In 1998, a scientist with significant conflicts of interest (he was being paid by a lawyer to build a lawsuit against the vaccine manufacturer, and he was developing a competing vaccine) falsified data to suggest that the MMR vaccine caused autism in children.[1] As a consequence, a worldwide campaign against childhood vaccinations began.[2] Over 200,000 children die of vaccine-preventable diseases each year.[3]

In another poignant example, geneticist Trofim Lysenko of the Soviet Union pedaled false ideas about crop genetics that led to the starvation of millions of countrymen when widespread crop failure caused a famine. He rejected the scientific ideas of genetics (that traits are inherited from parent plants to offspring plants) in favor of an outdated Lamarckian idea that you could force plants to change in their lifetimes based on environmental stimuli and that those changes would be passed on to offspring. Promising to drastically increase crop yields, his pseudoscience was enticing to the Soviet government. Claiming that he could turn one type of wheat into a hardier, winter-ready species, simply by changing the environment, the country planted it with drastic consequences.[4] These examples illustrate that fake science can cause very real consequences to our health and well-being.

Pseudoscience Causes Spiritual Harm

There is another devastating consequence of pseudoscience. Let's start with an email we received from one of our students. He reached out to us after graduating from BYU, having studied science. Here is what he said: "I have been going through a process of serious deconstruction of my Mormon faith. This process began when my very literal and dogmatic Mormon worldview was shattered as I became aware of the overwhelming evidence in support of evolution. This realization that everything I had been taught on this topic was likely wrong led me to question everything . . . to the point that I seriously doubt the very existence of God."[5]

In talking with this student, it was clear that he had been taught pseudoscientific ideas about how modern-day diversity came to be. He was *not* blaming the science of evolution for his fading testimony. Instead, he was disappointed in what he felt was deception from people in the Church who had used pseudoscience in place of real scientific explanations. He was reaching out to us for help in resolving his crisis. Tragically, he is not alone—not by a long shot. We see similar concerns among our students, for example, in relation to climate change, racial issues, and gender identity (covered in later chapters).

Unfortunately, we have encountered individuals who have the mistaken idea that providing pseudoscience will somehow save testimonies. They place the blame for declining religious devotion among the rising generation[6] squarely on science and believe that creating and teaching an alternative to science will not threaten testimonies and will help students avoid spiritual conflict. The very real danger is that, like our student above, when individuals find out that there is overwhelming scientific evidence to refute what they've been taught, they start to wonder about the truthfulness of other things they've been taught (for example, resurrection, the Atonement, and the reality of a Savior and a Heavenly Father). The result is absolutely heartbreaking.

Teach Science in Your Homes

What is the solution? Teach science (*real* science) in your homes, bathed in the light of the gospel, before your kids can hear it from someone else who might try to discount their beliefs (we've talked, for instance, about the all-too-common misconception that science is somehow atheistic in chapter 2). Let us liken this to another experience we had with the dean of Religious Education at BYU, Dr. Scott Esplin. He gave a fireside at Aspen Grove Family Camp in 2021,[7] where he talked about the Gospel Topics Essays that the Church has published in recent years. These essays address many somewhat controversial topics (for example, the Book of Mormon translation, Mother in Heaven, plural marriage, and race and the priesthood).[8] In light of all of the misinformation that is so easily accessible today via the internet, "The purpose of these essays . . . has been to gather accurate information from many different sources and publications and place it in the Gospel Topics section of ChurchofJesusChrist.org, where the material can more easily be accessed and studied by Church members and other interested parties."[9] Dr. Esplin went on to encourage all the parents in the audience to use these essays to teach their children about these topics *in the home, bathed in the light of the gospel*, so that their children would be equipped with truth *before* anyone else tried to challenge their faith using these topics.

You can almost think of educating ourselves and our children as a vaccination against Satan's attempts to destroy our faith. We are all increasingly concerned about the rising secularity in the youth. We suggest that the solution is to endow your children (and yourself) with the truth, with the *real* science and, if needed, seeking and offering ways to reconcile science with what we believe. By doing so, we provide protection against the fiery darts of the adversary (see 1 Nephi 15:24). He seeks to infuse doubt into our minds when we encounter something in science that seems to disagree with what we thought about the world. But we can arm ourselves and our children with the power of wisdom through learning *and* through faith (see Doctrine and Covenants 88:118).

We use a particular teaching approach for controversial science topics called the Reconciliation Model (RM), and it consists of the following steps: (1) acknowledge the existence of perceived conflict; (2) address the differences between science and religion (see chapter 1); (3) address the topic from a religious perspective (for example, examine what we know through the scriptures, Church teachings, or modern revelation); (4) discuss the cultural history (if there is any) that has led to the perceived conflict; and finally, (5) offer ways to reconcile the science with religious belief without compromising either and allowing for unknowns. We then teach and encourage students to seek out the scientific data and study the topic using good sources (see the explanation of the CRAAP test in chapter 1).

From extensive research we've conducted using the RM among both Latter-day Saint audiences and many other religious traditions, we have demonstrated that there is a way to reconcile science and religion that has no measurable harm on faith. Briefly, the RM utilizes cultural competence[10]—that is, acknowledging the cultural backgrounds of our students and presenting material in a nonthreatening way. This helps religious students feel more comfortable with science and to see the potential for compatibility between science and their religious views. We train educators to use the model and provide data to show that this approach is successful in increasing evolution acceptance (sometimes dramatically and, importantly, *without* any decrease in religious commitment). This model has been extensively tested among religious undergraduate biology students from multiple institutions,[11] undergraduate theology students,[12] public aquarium visitors,[13] and secondary biology and religious educators of various religious traditions.[14] In a real way, and with data to back it up, we can state that the Reconciliation Model protects the religious devotion of our students while increasing their acceptance of science, *and* we are doing it across the country with many faiths. It is exciting to see that science does not have to be a threat to testimonies and that it does not need to be explained away with pseudoscience.

Conclusion

It is in our homes where we can offer this coupled learning—learning through study and *also* through faith—and where we can give our children a complete knowledge of both temporal and spiritual things. A complete understanding of science in the context of religion can strengthen our faith before we encounter alternative ideas from the world that may shake our testimonies otherwise. We cannot solve these problems through pseudoscience. Truth can be found through the reconciliation of science and religion, and if we learn the real truths, they will not be in conflict.[15] As Brigham Young said, "All knowledge and wisdom and every good that the heart of man can desire is within the circuit and circle of the faith we have embraced."[16]

CHAPTER 5

COMFORT WITH UNCERTAINTY

The final point in our discussion on reconciling science and religion is that we need to be *comfortable with uncertainty.* Feeling uncertain about something brings discomfort and a desire to resolve it; uncertainty is generally unsettling to humans. This is especially true if the uncertainty contains risks and unknown outcomes and if we cannot judge the likelihood of our making successful decisions because we lack critical information.[1] This uncertainty can lead to reactionary responses, largely instinctual, and irrational, subconscious decision-making.[2] If we manage to overcome our reactionary responses and consider the evidence more rationally, we may avoid drawing rash conclusions. To do this, we must learn to reserve judgment and accept some uncertainty. In this chapter, we will discuss the following:

- The necessary role of uncertainty for scientific progress
- The difference between scientific progress and established scientific knowledge
- The danger of being dogmatic from both a scientific and a religious perspective
- How to become comfortable with uncertainty such that it allows our testimonies to grow

Our goals in this discussion are, first, to help us recognize that in both science and religion we still have much to learn. Second, we need to learn to feel comfortable with not having all the information right now. Third, we should allow ourselves the time to learn and progress without having to make a decision that places science and religion at odds with one another.

Scientific Progress Depends on Uncertainty

Let's start with a thinking exercise. How much uncertainty in scientific understanding is there? What role (if any) does uncertainty play in the process of science? The first is fairly easy to answer as long as we have a good dose of humility. There are definitely a lot of questions about the natural world that we still don't have complete answers for. For example,

- What particles in the environment trigger many autoimmune diseases (for instance, diabetes, rheumatoid arthritis, or lupus)?
- Why does the COVID-19 vaccine offer immunity for only a short period?
- Why are *Homo sapiens* (us) the only species left among our human-like ancestors?

The list could go on and on. But for each of these, we do know a great deal. For example, we know that

- autoimmune diseases are caused when the body produces an antibody to its own tissue and that the antibody is triggered by something in the environment.[3]
- all vaccines prompt the body to produce immunity and keep a memory of it for future protection.[4]
- at least three other *Homo* species overlapped our existence.[5]

The point is that when scientists say they are "uncertain," it does not mean that they "know nothing." So what role does uncertainty play? Let's look at a great example.

Have you ever wondered how a seed, weighing less than an ounce, can grow into a tree weighing hundreds of pounds? Most of our students naïvely suggest that the plant is "eating" nutrients in the soil. When confronted with the reasoning, "If plants have to gain hundreds of pounds of weight from the soil, why doesn't the soil disappear?," students are a little stumped. This was true of early scientists as well. A scientist in the 1600s, Jan Baptista van Helmont, set out to solve this conundrum. In his own words, he stated:

> I took an earthen pot and in it placed 200 pounds of earth which had been dried out in an oven. This I moistened with rain water, and in it planted a shoot of willow which weighed five pounds. When five years had passed the tree which grew from it weighed 169 pounds and about three ounces. The earthen pot was wetted whenever it was necessary with rain or distilled water only. It was very large, and was sunk in the ground, and had a tin plated iron lid with many holes punched in it, which covered the edge of the pot to keep air-borne dust from mixing with the earth. I did not keep track of the weight of the leaves which fell in each of the four autumns. Finally, I dried out the earth in the pot once more, and found the same 200 pounds, less about 2 ounces. Thus, 164 pounds of wood, bark, and roots had arisen from water alone.[6]

Van Helmont concluded that the mass of the tree was not coming from the soil (which had lost only two ounces) but from the water. His theory seemed to make sense, given his experiment. However, there still remained a lot of uncertainty. Trees do not appear to be made from water alone. In fact, later analysis would reveal that the primary structure of a tree comes from cellulose (a type of carbohydrate that is made of carbon, hydrogen, and oxygen) and that trees release oxygen gas. Many key experiments, dating back to the 1700s, helped scientists discover the full mechanisms of plant growth.[7] A rather interesting one in 1941 relates directly to Van Helmont's experiment. Researchers used oxygen isotopes[8] to track the oxygen in water (H_2O) to see if it went directly into the cellulose. They were surprised to find that it did not. Instead, the oxygen from the water was being released into the air as oxygen gas.[9] So where was all that oxygen (and carbon) coming from if not from the soil? It turns out that plants consume carbon dioxide from the atmosphere and that this gas is what ultimately turned into cellulose.[10] In other words, plants get almost *all* of their mass from the air! Thus, through repeated experimentation, we have become more certain about this particular process. But it was the uncertainty that pushed science along.

We could share many other examples in which scientific understanding has been refined based on new evidence prompted by uncertainty. A recent example provides an excellent illustration. First, an important distinction needs to be made, which was laid out beautifully by physicist Pierre Hohenberg. He proposed that there should be a "distinction between the activity of scientists and the product of that activity: the former is denoted (lower-case) science and the latter (upper-case) Science."[11] The "big-S Science" to which he refers is "collective, public knowledge . . . universal and free of contradiction . . . nevertheless bathed in ignorance and subject to change."[12] Whereas, "little-s science" is messy, constantly evolving and changing as a beautiful process of discovery. In the world's experience with COVID-19, this distinction was sometimes ignored. The "big-S Science" is plentiful: We know through germ theory that SARS-CoV-2 is a disease-causing agent that results in the symptoms we see as COVID-19 infection.[13] We know that our bodies, in response to a disease-causing agent, create antibodies to fight it through a process called adaptive immunity. We know that a vaccine can mimic a disease-causing agent such that the body creates "memory" of infection and therefore immunity. If all goes perfectly, we will not catch the same disease-causing agent twice.[14]

The "little-s science" includes the discovery of many things, such as the novel mechanisms of COVID-19; the effectiveness of pharmaceutical treatments like ivermectin, monoclonal antibodies, or remdesivir; the various features of each new variant; the design of an mRNA vaccine; the effectiveness of the vaccine at prompting lasting immunity; and so on. The interesting thing about this pandemic is that it has taken place at an unprecedented time in history, when "little-s science" is watched in real time through social, local, and national media, and when everyone is a witness to the process of discovery. In days past, it was difficult to get "little-s science" to the public in any meaningful and efficient way; thus, most people were only aware of "big-S Science'—when consensus had been reached and a relatively large amount of information was known with surety. Now, however, people are watching the messy, and sometimes disconcerting, process of "little-s science," and it seems that many are quite uncomfortable with it. Could this be because of a misunderstanding of the nature of uncertainty in the process? Interestingly, researchers have found that when people encounter information about a topic that seems to contradict their worldview, they tend to assume science is useless in answering questions about that topic (called scientific impotence discounting).[15]

Balancing an understanding of the role uncertainty plays in the scientific process with the tendency to see uncertainty as a reason to throw out science is sometimes tricky. But a good understanding of the difference between the *process* (little-s) and the *product* (big-S) of science can help us feel more comfortable with scientific uncertainty. Remember, nothing is completely "proven" in science, but this does not mean science knows nothing. All information (scientific and nonscientific) may be viewed with a critical eye. It is not wrong to question information that we hear; in fact, doing so is critical to discovering truth. With the abundance of information at our fingertips in today's digital age, it behooves us to move forward with patience, temperance, caution, and reasonable skepticism. Scrutiny drives a dynamic process of discovery and refinement toward "big-S Science," which then has the power to explain the natural world and to improve our lives.

Dogmatism Stifles Progress

Dogmatism is to be "certain that your beliefs are right and that others should accept them, without paying attention to evidence or other opinions."[16] When people are dogmatic, they are drawing a conclusion that is untested and incapable of change. They are unwilling to listen and, therefore, unwilling to learn. We should avoid becoming dogmatic (that is, irrationally insistent) about particular beliefs or claims.

President Dieter F. Uchtdorf warned us that "so often the 'truths' we tell ourselves are merely fragments of the truth, and sometimes they're not really the truth at all. . . . When the opinions or 'truths' of others contradict our own, instead of considering the possibility that there could be information that might be helpful and augment or complement what we know, we often jump to conclusions or make assumptions that the other person is misinformed, mentally challenged, or even intentionally trying to deceive."[17] This response is a result of pride and it is perpetuated by the great deceiver, even Satan, who hopes to prevent us from finding truth (Doctrine and Covenants 50:3).

Dogmatism can have dangerous consequences, and we've seen these consequences played out in the history of science on some tragic occasions when scientists were unwilling to consider new information. One such occasion happened in the development of germ theory (the idea that microscopic living things could cause disease). A young physician by the name of Ignaz Philipp Semmelweis was working as a gynecologist in the mid-1800s. He noticed a stark difference in death rates of mothers afflicted with "childbed fever" who were cared for at one clinic versus another. One clinic was primarily operated by practicing physicians and had higher death rates than the clinic used primarily for midwifery training. Through a series of experiments, he concluded that the causal agent of disease was coming from corpses that were being examined by the physicians prior to gynecological exams. The midwives never participated in such procedures. Semmelweis instituted a handwashing policy in the first clinic (asking medical personnel to wash their hands in what would be chlorine bleach today). Within a few short months, he saw a 90% decrease in deaths from childbed fever. Dogmatism, however, prevented the scientific community from accepting Semmelweis's clear data on handwashing practices. It took at least a decade before others like Louis Pasteur began to put the pieces together for germ theory, long after Semmelweis's death.[18]

President Russell M. Nelson pointed out that this principle of handwashing was revealed by the Lord more than three thousand years ago to the children of Israel in Leviticus 15, where the Lord counsels the people to wash their bodies, clothing, and beds after they have a "running issue out of [their] flesh" (Leviticus 15:2). President Nelson then states, "These scriptures are in complete harmony with modern medical guidelines. But during those many millennia, how many mothers needlessly perished? How many children suffered because man's quest for knowledge had failed to incorporate the word of the Lord?"[19] Sometimes, in truly dogmatic fashion, scientists assume that science is the only way of knowing truth. As Thomas Burnett, previous director of the AAAS Dialogue on Science Ethics and Religion,[20] explains,

> It is one thing to celebrate science for its achievements and remarkable ability to explain a wide variety of phenomena in the natural world. But to claim there is nothing knowable outside the scope of science would be similar to a successful fisherman saying that whatever he can't catch in his nets does not exist. Once you accept that science is the only source of human knowledge, you have adopted a philosophical position (scientism) that cannot be verified, or falsified, by science itself. It is, in a word, unscientific.[21]

Dogmatism exists in religion as well. Many might incorrectly assume that truth *only* comes through religious revelations. Take, for example, this statement by Henry Morris, a famous Young Earth creationist who founded the Institute for Creation Research: "Since nothing in the world has been created since the end of the creation period, everything has then been created by means or processes which are no longer in operation and which we therefore cannot study by any of the means of science. We are limited exclusively to divine revelation as to the date of creation, the duration of creation, the method of creation, and every other question concerning creation."[22]

Is this true? Do we, as Latter-day Saints, believe this? Certainly, we do not. We believe that God is the same yesterday, today, and forever (see Mormon 9:9). He does not use different methods today than He did during the Creation. Thus, for us, it follows that science is a way we can study His creations.

Comfort with Uncertainty Allows Room for Our Testimonies to Grow

There is an old Indian proverb that illustrates a relevant point.[23] It goes something like this: Six blind men come upon an elephant. Each grasping a different part, they imagine the truth of an elephant quite differently. The one touching the side imagines an elephant like a wall, the one who grabs the trunk imagines it like a snake, the one who grabs the tail imagines a rope, and so on. The men argue back and forth about what the elephant really looks like. All of them are partially correct, but all of them are also wrong. None of them have actually seen the elephant.

The point of the story is that none of us, at this point, know the truth of all things. We have been promised that someday we will (see Doctrine and Covenants 101:32), but until then, we can be patient. As the Apostle Paul described, "For now we see through a glass, darkly" (1 Corinthians 13:12). Just like the blind men in the story of the elephant, we do not have a complete knowledge yet. And that is perfectly okay, even part of the plan. In fact, we believe that there are many great and important things yet to be revealed to us (see Articles of Faith 1:9) and that if anything is "virtuous, lovely, or of good report or praiseworthy, we seek after these things" (Articles of Faith 1:13). The point is to have patience. When something seems contradictory, be patient and wait for more truth to be revealed. Better yet, seek out more truth. As President Uchtdorf commented, "I believe that our Father in Heaven is pleased with His children when they use their talents and mental faculties to earnestly discover truth. Over the centuries many wise men and women—through logic, reason, scientific inquiry, and, yes, through inspiration—have discovered truth. These discoveries have enriched mankind, improved our lives, and inspired joy, wonder, and awe."[24]

How many of us would claim to know all there is to know about the gospel? Probably no one. Yet how often do we feel that if we do not have certain, unshakeable knowledge, we are somehow less faithful or in danger of losing our testimonies? We sometimes set up a culture that demands that we "know" the truth of all things. Likewise, how many of us would claim that we know all of science? Hopefully none of us. If we thought we knew everything, the scientific enterprise would come to a screeching halt. It is okay to be uncertain. It is okay to not know everything right now. It is okay to be constantly working on our testimonies, growing in the gospel, increasing our understanding, and working out how the book of nature goes together with the book of God.

Conclusion

Uncertainty is a hallmark of both science and religion. It is what drives us forward and makes us seek out more scientific and spiritual truth. Feeling comfortable with not knowing the truth of all things and avoiding dogmatism can bring exceptional freedom. When we are open-minded, we invite further light and knowledge that the Lord wishes to bestow upon us. Most importantly, by following the teachings of our Savior, who is "the way, the truth, and the life" (John 14:6), we can be guided by the Holy Ghost in seeking truth. And by having patience, we can avoid doubting our faith when things we learn seem to conflict with our beliefs. Lastly, if learning scientific theories puts your faith in jeopardy, choose your faith. Choose your faith until you can better understand the science (or until science can provide better explanations). We have a testimony that both religious and scientific truths can exist in harmony.

SECTION II

"STICKY TOPICS" IN THE LIFE SCIENCES

CHAPTER 6

EVOLUTION

When people hear the word *evolution*, they often think of the idea that monkeys transformed into humans or that a blob-like, single-celled creature in a bubbling pool decided to sprout legs and crawl onto land. However, both of those ideas are flawed. Scientifically, evolution is "descent with modification." "Descent" means that all living things on earth (both plants and animals) share a common ancestor, but it does not mean that one animal or plant changes or morphs into another. "With modification" means that, over time, the genetic composition of populations of living things changes and these changes can lead to significant modifications in how these living things appear. (This definition is simplified but sufficient for our conversation.) The theory of evolution encompasses complex processes that cannot be covered in full here; we will, however, carefully illustrate what science, as a way of knowing, suggests about *when* life came to be and *how* it came to appear as it does today. *Why* life is here and *who* brought it into being are religious questions. When coupled together, a more complete understanding of *why*, *who*, *how*, and *when* is possible.

What about Evolution Needs Reconciliation?

When it comes to the gospel and evolution, there are three main questions we often hear: How does evolution fit with the Creation? Do we really see change in "kinds"? And if humans evolved, where do Adam and Eve fit in?

What Has the Church Said about Evolution?

Before we jump into the science, we want to first approach the Church's official stance on evolution. Members and leaders of our Church have made a variety of statements regarding evolution, both in favor of and against organic evolution. But we will start with official statements made by the First Presidency, specifically regarding the origin of man, from 1909 and 1925. Created under the direction of President Joseph F. Smith, the 1909 statement reads:

> It is held by some that Adam was not the first man upon this earth and that the original human being was a development from lower orders of the animal creation. These, however, are the theories of men. The word of the Lord declared that Adam was "the first man of all men" (Moses 1:34), and we are therefore duty bound to regard him as the primal parent of our race. It was shown to the brother of Jared that all men were created in the *beginning* after the image of God; whether we take this to mean the spirit or the body, or both, it commits us to the same conclusion: Man began life as a human being, in the likeness of our Heavenly Father.[1]

Following this statement, President Smith cautioned teachers about making statements regarding "how much of evolution is true, or how much is false." In a follow-up statement in 1925, the basic principles of humans' origin[2] were reiterated. Additionally, the statement read:

> All men and women are in the similitude of the universal Father and Mother, and are literally sons and daughters of Deity. . . . Man is the child of God, formed in the divine image and endowed with divine attributes, and even as the infant son of an earthly father and mother is capable in due time of becoming a man, so that undeveloped offspring of celestial parentage is capable, by experience through ages and aeons, of evolving into a God.

Neither statement confirmed or denied the claims of

evolutionary science but simply underscored humankind's relationship to God and affirmed His role in Creation. Though conflicting views persisted among prominent Church leaders, President Heber J. Grant urged them to "leave Geology, Biology, Archaeology and Anthropology, no one of which has to do with the salvation of the souls of mankind, to scientific research, while we magnify our calling in the realm of the Church."[3]

More recently, in 2016, the Church published a statement focused on evolution (including the evolution of humans) in its magazine to youth, stating:

> The Church has no official position on the theory of evolution. Organic evolution, or changes to species' inherited traits over time, is a matter for scientific study. Nothing has been revealed concerning evolution. Though the details of what happened on earth before Adam and Eve, including how their bodies were created, have not been revealed, our teachings regarding man's origin are clear and come from revelation.
>
> Before we were born on earth, we were spirit children of heavenly parents, with bodies in their image. God directed the creation of Adam and Eve and placed their spirits in their bodies.[4]

The most recent summary of the Church's position on evolution can be found on the Church's website in the Church History Topics section, under the heading "Organic Evolution." This essay documents the varying views of Church leaders over time:

> Latter-day Saints and their leaders found themselves on both sides of this issue. James E. Talmage and John A. Widtsoe, two professional scientists who became Apostles, regarded scientific discovery of truth as evidence of God's use of natural laws to govern the universe. Meanwhile, Apostle and future Church President Joseph Fielding Smith believed that the Biblical account of the Creation did not allow for the long spans required for species to

> multiply through evolution. . . . Henry Eyring, a prominent scientist and Sunday School general board member, welcomed evidence of evolutionary change and reiterated the teachings of Brigham Young, who taught that the gospel encompassed all truth, scientific or otherwise. In 1965, Church President David O. McKay worked with Bertrand F. Harrison, a botany professor at Brigham Young University, to foster greater understanding between Saints with differing viewpoints on evolution.[5]

So while individual Church leaders have frequently shared their personal beliefs both in favor of and in opposition to evolution, these statements do not represent Church doctrine. The Church is effectively neutral toward matters of evolution. With that in mind, we would like to tackle three topics surrounding evolution from a scientific perspective and then offer ways in which the scientific explanations can be reconciled with our belief in God as the Divine Creator.

The Creation

The Creation, as told in Genesis, Moses, and Abraham, is a beautiful testament to God's creative powers and love for His children. However, these scriptures were not meant to be a scientific textbook on how the Creation took place.[6] The Creation accounts in our sacred texts do teach some important truths about the natural world: (1) God created the earth, the land and the seas, the heavens and the night sky, the sun and the moon (Genesis 1:3–10, 14–19); (2) God created all living things—the herbs of the field, the fishes in the sea, the fowls in the air, and the beasts of the field (Genesis 1:11–13, 20–25); and (3) God created man and woman in His own image (Genesis 1:26–27). The details of *how* these creations occurred are very sparse (again, because the purpose of these records was not to illustrate the scientific mechanisms). Yet we gain some unique insight in the book of Abraham.

In Abraham 4:21, the Gods (Jesus Christ under the direction of Heavenly Father; see Abraham 4:1; Mosiah 4:2; Doctrine and Covenants 14:9) are creating life. The passage reads, "The Gods *prepared* the waters that they might bring forth great whales, and every living creature that moveth. . . . And the Gods saw that they would be obeyed, and that *their plan was good*" (emphasis added). Isn't this an interesting way of describing the Creation? The Gods had a plan for the Creation, and They organized the earth in a way that would accomplish Their plan. Does this scripture leave room for the idea that They established natural laws and provided natural materials for life to emerge through the processes of evolution, knowing that it would happen exactly as it did? Could it be that They patiently watched to see if They would be obeyed, to see if Their plan was good, to see if They had put it all in place correctly? This is just one potential way to view the Creation, but one that we find helpful to consider.

If this is the case, do we have evidence for a Creation orchestrated through evolution? It turns out that science provides a lot of evidence that evolution did (and continues to) occur, suggesting that evolution is a possible mechanism of creation. This then leads to an interesting question: If God used evolution to bring about His creations, how long (in our earthly accounting of time) did the Creation of the world take? This is a question for which science can offer a potential answer. Briefly, we know how long ago rocks formed by looking at the presence of isotopes (variations of elements that decay at a predictable rate and turn into other elements), their proportions, and their arrangements. The oldest rocks found on earth (along with collaborative evidence from meteors and moon rocks) suggest that the earth is around 4.6 billion years old.[7] We can also look to science to learn when the first life-forms appeared. Based on fossil evidence of bacterial-type colonies embedded in rocks, scientists have determined that the first living things began to appear at least by 1.9 billion years ago and possibly even before, at 3.4–3.6 billion years ago.[8] Thus, if God prepared evolution as a mechanism for creation, then this creation presumably began with this first life-form, which then transformed through generations, by God's plan, into the beautiful array of living things we see today.

Here are a few simple illustrations of how, according to scientists, evolution from a single ancestor occurred. First, one of the most important pieces of evidence comes from DNA, the genetic material inside our cells. Not only do all living things on earth contain DNA, but they also all read DNA the same way. This means that if you took a gene (a gene is a piece of DNA that codes for a specific characteristic) from a jellyfish, like the green fluorescent protein (the protein that allows them to glow) and you put it into a rabbit, the rabbit will read the gene the same way, produce the same protein, and glow in the dark.[9] Likewise, if you put that protein in a plant or even a human, they would also glow, because all life on earth, including humans, read DNA the same way. This is strong evidence that we all shared a common beginning. Further, if you compare all the genes between organisms, you'll find that the more closely related the organisms, the more genes they share and the more likely they will share mutations or unique differences in these genes. For example, all mammals carry the necessary genes for making vitamin C; however, primates have a mutation that makes it impossible to make vitamin C. The same mutation in all of these primates is in the exact same gene.[10] This strongly suggests that these primates share a common ancestor who gained this mutation and then passed it on.

Second, the similarities in body structure of humans and animals hint at an evolutionary past. For example, if you look inside the forearm of a human, you will see a long humerus bone, stretching from the shoulder to the elbow, two shorter bones (radius and ulna) stretching from the elbow to the wrist, a bunch of little cube-shaped bones in the wrist, and then small, thin bones that make up your hands and fingers. If we share common ancestry with other living things, we would find these same bones in the arms of other four-legged animals such as frogs, cats, bats, whales, and even dinosaurs (see figure 6.1).

Not only do we find these same bones in many animals but, interestingly, we also see bones in some animals that no longer serve a purpose—like pelvic bones and hand bones in whales, and a tailbone in humans. These are called vestiges, which are "evolutionary leftovers," evidence that the whale's ancestors once had legs and fingers and the human's ancestors once had a tail. We carry a rich history of our relatives in our bodies.

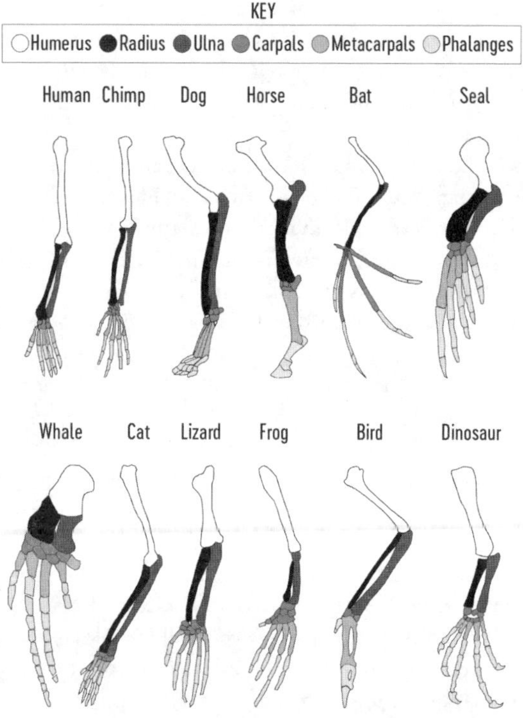

Figure 6.1. Animal Limb Bones

Third, fossils offer excellent evidence of the evolutionary process. Not all areas of the earth have fossils due to the recycling of the earth's crust (for example, through erosion, tectonic-plate subduction, and volcanic activity), but fossils are still plentiful. Many of them show wonderful transitions between organisms, such as the *Archaeopteryx*, a feathered dinosaur that lived in the late Jurassic period 150 million years ago. These fossils show the transition of non-avian dinosaurs (like the velociraptors in *Jurassic Park*) into the feathered birds we have today. In fact, one scientist team is actively trying to turn the "dinosaur genes" that chickens still possess back on to make a "chicken-o-saurus." They have successfully produced chickens with rudimentary teeth and claws.[11]

Fourth, we can look at embryonic development. The scientific term for this development is *ontogeny*: the stages all organisms go through from conception to adulthood. In examining the development of the embryo of animals with spines (vertebrates), including humans, we see fascinating moments when *all* of these embryos develop gills and tails (see figure 6.2). But as the embryos continue to develop, these features are either lost or retained according to the species. For example, fish retain their gills, but the gill arches of the human embryo form a jaw and ear bones.[12] Similarly, cats retain their tail while the human embryo's tail becomes reduced and forms the coccyx.[13] We even see rudimentary hind limbs develop in whale and dolphin embryos.[14] To science, this supports that life on earth evolved through small changes to developmental pathways.

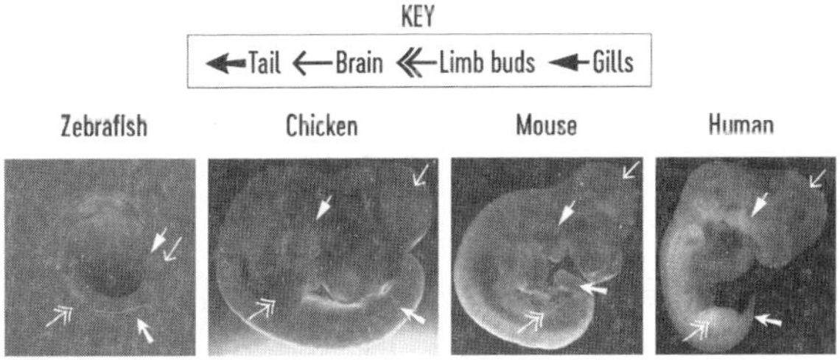

Figure 6.2. Embryos

Fifth, the distribution of fossils and living organisms on earth, termed *biogeography*, provides compelling evidence for how they got there. Earth's geography has been tumultuous since its beginning. As tectonic plates separate, they also move and separate the plants and animals that inhabit them at that time. Today we can see these patterns in living species. For example, flightless birds (like ostriches, emus, and so on) and marsupials share similar DNA and anatomy but exist on several different continents and islands. How did this happen if they cannot fly? Evidence shows that a common ancestor of both flightless birds and marsupials existed across the southern portion of Pangea (a supercontinent from 250 million years ago) that broke apart, forming today's continents. Members of each group were separated when the land separated and gave rise to each new species of flightless birds and marsupials that we see today.[15] Additionally, fossils show where ancient oceans once were, how dry land came to be, and how that land was broken up to form the continents and islands of today. Biogeographical patterns of plants and animals provide more scientific evidence for evolution.

We could keep giving more evidence of our evolutionary heritage, but then this would turn into a science textbook. Suffice it to say, scientists have not come lightly to the conclusion that all organisms evolved on earth. They have accumulated mountains of evidence that suggest that this is a strong and highly plausible explanation. This does not need to diminish your belief in our Heavenly Father as the Creator.

Many believing scientists (including us) have thought deeply about how to reconcile the evidence we see through science with our conviction that God is the Creator. There is a spectrum of beliefs regarding the Creation and evolution, which we partly introduced in chapter 2.[16] We will share the viewpoints in more detail here and discuss each belief's potential compatibility with the scientific evidence:

- **Day-Age Creationism:** This belief generally suggests that the "days" of Creation described in scriptural accounts represent periods of time of unknown length. In this respect, it may allow for the gradual creation of animal and plant life that would leave behind the evidence we see (similar DNA, fossils, speciation, and so on). Potential issues of compatibility only arise if one stipulates that the creative periods had to occur in the exact order described and cannot overlap (for instance, plants would have had to be completely created before animals began, which is incompatible with fossil evidence) or that once the Creation was done, all creation ceased (which also conflicts with current evidence).

- **Progressive Creationism:** Those who espouse this idea believe that each organism, each new species, each new kind, was a special creation of God. Certainly God could have played a role in each species' creation, directing and creating each phase of the evolutionary story. Potential issues of compatibility arise if we do not allow for each incremental life-form for which we have fossil evidence.
- **Theistic Evolution:** This idea suggests that evolution occurred exactly as the scientific evidence suggests but that God was actively directing the process with clear purpose and care for His creations.[17] As far as we can see, there are no issues of compatibility with the scientific evidence unless one chooses to exclude humans from this process, applying a "special creation" status to us.
- **Deistic Evolution:** This idea acknowledges the existence of God and His role in instigating the creation of the universe but then assumes no direct divine interference in the process. Again, we see no issue of compatibility with science. However, unlike some adherents of deistic evolution who do not believe there was Godly purpose or care, we believe that God had a clear purpose in creating this earth.

All of these viewpoints (taking into account the caveats we discussed) are completely compatible with both scientific evidence and our doctrine, and none of them limit the power of God. We only place limits upon God's power when we require that His creation fit our own personal views or when we try to suppress the views of others. Thus, regardless of whether God played an active, orderly, interventionist role in every step of the Creation (as in day-age creationism) or was involved in each miniscule step (as in progressive creationism), or whether He prepared the earth and its laws and then allowed the process to take place according to His design (as in theistic or deistic evolution), we know that He was deeply involved. We believe that the evidence we find for evolution is just evidence of His divine hand.

Change in "Kinds"

Genesis 1:24 reads, "And God said let the earth bring forth the living creature after his kind." Some interpret this to mean there is no evolution between "kinds" (that is, there is no single common ancestor for life on earth). "Kinds" is an interesting word used in the scriptures, not found in science. From a religious perspective, we know very little about "kinds." We see the word used in the Creation account (Genesis 1:12, 21) and in the account of Noah when he was commanded to take of each kind onto the ark (Genesis 6:20). But we have little information about what a "kind" is *and* about what it means to "bring forth" living creatures. Some believe "kinds" are synonymous with "species" and thus species have never changed or arisen since the Creation (this notion is somewhat problematic from a scientific perspective because *species* is difficult to define). Others broaden "kinds" to something beyond what is commonly defined as a species, such as all cat species (including lions, tigers, and housecats) or all types of whales (including blue, baleen, beluga, and more). So perhaps changes in species are okay, but could a single common ancestor billions of years ago have led, through evolution, to larger groups of life? Do these scriptures really place limits on God's creative processes? These are questions for which we do not have any scriptural guidance or modern revelation. But science shows that evolutionary changes have occurred at all levels.

Since "kinds" doesn't appear to have a scientific equivalent, for the sake of our discussion, we'd like to focus on species. A *species* is something that continues to be debated in science because there are so many ways to define the term. The definition with which you are probably most familiar is the "biological species," defined as organisms that can reproduce with each other to produce living, fertile offspring. This concept is flawed, however, when you consider asexual species, like bacteria, or species that *can* do this but don't actually meet in the wild, like lions and tigers. Another way to classify species is by similarity due to ancestry (in terms of DNA and anatomy), called "phylogenetic species." This definition, however, is difficult to apply to fossil creatures for which we have no DNA or only partial anatomy. Yet another way to define species is by the creatures' ecology—where they live, what they eat, and so on. This is, not surprisingly, called "ecological species." But this definition too has several flaws, one of which is that it doesn't account for when an organism changes its ecology during its own lifetime, as in the case of a caterpillar. Thus, even scientists struggle to define species in any one way; but using the ways in which these different definitions agree, scientists can define groups of animals and their common ancestry.

Now let's talk about *how* evolution happens and if the process could lead to the emergence of new species. Remember, evolution is defined as any change in the genetic composition within a population. For example, if a population of sandy-colored mice move to an area with predominantly black lava rock, those mice born with darker fur will likely blend in better, survive longer, and reproduce more; the composition of the genes in that population would thus gradually change so that the mice's fur goes from mostly sandy to mostly dark.[18] The mechanism for this change is called "natural selection," and it is probably the mechanism with which you are most familiar. Individuals with characteristics that lead to better reproduction (and survival) pass those characteristics to their offspring. Other mechanisms that change the genetic composition of a population include genetic drift (random genetic changes over time, accentuated in small populations), gene flow (when organisms move between populations), mutation (when the DNA sequence of genes is actually changed), and nonrandom mating (when individuals choose a mate based on some characteristic rather than by chance alone). All of these mechanisms are highly likely to occur at some point. Thus, populations are continuously changing—that is, evolving.

The question then is whether these somewhat smaller changes within populations of a single species can lead to diversification into different species. Science says yes. Mountains, rivers, oceans, and so on can function as barriers that isolate populations that then continue to evolve under different environmental conditions. Additionally, modes of communication and reproduction can also divide populations. If some frogs or fireflies start to prefer a different sexual signal (like a faster call or a brighter flash), while the rest of the population does not, then those creatures that prefer something different could become genetically different through the mechanisms of evolution. If these physical or behavioral barriers persist long enough, over many thousands or millions of years, these populations could eventually become different species.

The processes that cause small changes are the same processes that cause these large changes; they are just spread over a longer period—longer than a human lifespan, so we cannot witness it. We can only look for evidence left behind in genetics or anatomy. For example, scientists hypothesize that whales and hippos evolved from the same ancestor. There are several lines of evidence for this; there are DNA similarities, for instance, and one of the strongest pieces of evidence is the astragalus (a unique ankle bone) that exists in both modern hippos *and* in whale ancestors (ones with primitive hind legs).[19] This pattern of change has repeated itself millions of times since the start of life on earth.[20] So it appears, at least by analyzing our current scientific evidence, that all species on our planet today, including those preserved in all known fossils, emerged from a single common ancestor. It appears that whether God intervened all along the way or He set the plan in motion and stepped back to watch His work, He began with a single template, the common ancestor of all life on earth.[21]

Adam and Eve

Scripture teaches us that we were first created spiritually, then physically (Moses 3; Doctrine and Covenants 29:31–32). Through modern revelation, we know that "Adam, our great progenitor, 'the first man,' was, like Christ, a pre-existent spirit, and, like Christ, he took upon him an appropriate body, the body of a man, and so became a 'living soul.'"[22] Science can provide possible insight on where this body might have come from, but how God breathed life into it is not scientifically testable. Science cannot tell you about the soul that inhabits your body, where it came from, or why it is there. As was quoted previously, "The Church has no official position on the theory of evolution . . . including how [Adam's and Eve's] bodies were created."[23] Additional insight was offered by President Spencer W. Kimball when he stated, "The Creators breathed into their nostrils the breath of life and man and woman became living souls. We don't know exactly how their coming into this world happened, and when we're able to understand it the Lord will tell us."[24]

Thus, regarding Adam and Eve, we cannot offer a sufficient explanation beyond what we have stated here; we lack modern revelation concerning the exact timing of when Adam and Eve lived, where their bodies came from, or how they relate to other prehuman species that existed on earth. Could Adam's and Eve's bodies have evolved? Were Adam and Eve a special case of creation that did not evolve? Were Adam and Eve transplanted from another sphere? We feel it is important to remain open-minded about the science of human origins while maintaining a firm and unshakeable testimony that God created Adam and Eve and that we are God's children.

Does evidence for evolution of the human species exist?

Yes. We will not go into extensive detail about human evolution (we can recommend several great books about the history of *Homo sapiens*, our species[25]). Briefly, there are at least 21 known species of hominin (ancestors of our species) that once existed on our planet dating back 5 million years. Modern *Homo sapiens* first appeared around 300,000 years ago.[26] Regarding the evidence for human evolution, we are often asked how we know that a specimen, such as a skull, that has been discovered is really from a different species and not just a representative of some extreme variation in our species. Well, first, we usually do not classify a new species based on *one* skull, but many representatives. For example, we currently have more than 300 *Homo neanderthal* specimens,[27] dating from 400,000 to 40,000 years ago in Europe and Asia, and at least 18 different members of *Homo naledi*, the latest hominin discovery,[28] who lived between 335,000 and 236,000 years ago in South Africa, both of which existed at the time *Homo sapiens* evolved. Second, these specimens are physically different enough from us (using the phylogenetic-species concept) to be considered a different species.

Given the evidence, science suggests the human body is a product of evolution. However, how this fits (or doesn't fit) with our divine natures and the plan of salvation is left to you. We can only offer a spectrum of possibilities on which you can place your beliefs. One of the best statements describing this spectrum comes from correspondence from the First Presidency (then under the direction of President Joseph F. Smith) to the priesthood organizations of the Church: "Whether the mortal bodies of man evolved in natural processes to present perfection, through the direction and power of God; whether the first parents of our generations, Adam and Eve, were transplanted from another sphere, with immortal tabernacles, which became corrupted through sin and the partaking of natural foods, in the process of time; whether they were born here in mortality, as other mortals have been, are questions not fully answered in the revealed word of God."[29]

So the spectrum spans from special creation to the transplantation of a fully formed Adam and Eve into this world, where other organisms already existed (even other hominid organisms, as the scientific evidence suggests), to the evolution of their mortal bodies (the same as other organisms) into which their spirits were placed.

The Biological Basis of "Race"

We cannot talk of evolution without taking a moment to talk about race from a biological perspective, since it is a natural area of interest when discussing human evolution. From a scientific viewpoint, our species is under the same evolutionary pressures as other species. Thus, humans show a diversity of traits,[30] including differences in complexion (for example, skin, eye, and hair color) or physical features (most often facial[31]). These differences have been used to separate our species into races. The human species, however, is comparatively quite young and so good at mixing their genes across the globe that races are not scientifically diagnosable. Humans are so similar genetically, even among the most different-looking humans imaginable, that it is actually impossible to use a diversity of genetic markers to draw clear lines between human races.[32] In short, looking at DNA alone, we would be hard-pressed to determine a "race."[33]

Conclusion

As we learn about evolution, if we perceive conflict with our religious beliefs, we can take comfort in the counsel of President Russell M. Nelson: "There is no conflict between science and religion. Conflict only arises from an incomplete knowledge of either science or religion, or both. . . . All truth is part of the gospel of Jesus Christ. Whether truth comes from a scientific laboratory or by revelation from the Lord, it is compatible."[34] With this assurance, we can carefully acquire all the experience and data possible to answer questions that might seed doubt in our testimonies if left unconfronted. If evolution is one of those questions, then exploring the data for evolution need not be scary. As President Dallin H. Oaks counseled us, "We are supposed to learn by both reason and revelation, and that does not happen when we compartmentalize science and religion. Our searching should be disciplined by human reason and also enlightened by divine revelation. In the end, truth has only one content and one source, and it encompasses both science and religion."[35]

Patiently applying knowledge from religion and science, revelation and reason, is the suggested path to resolving the conflict that evolution may bring to our current viewpoints and that can challenge our testimonies and those of our loved ones.

CHAPTER 7

HEALTH AND MEDICAL SCIENCE

We all wonder how to live healthily, prolong life, and generate posterity. In the United States, the Department of Health and Human Services (HHS) receives more than a quarter of the total government budget.[1] HHS invests about a third of its discretionary funding to basic medical research through the National Institutes of Health,[2] the largest biomedical research organization in the world.[3] Clearly, the goal of advancing the health and wellness of our society is a high priority in the US and elsewhere. As Latter-day Saints, we believe that modern medical breakthroughs are tools to bring about God's miracles. As we use the truths of the everlasting gospel as a guiding framework, we can faithfully pursue ways to improve our health, our lives, and our families.

What about Health and Medical Science Needs Reconciliation?

We will address three main questions related to health and medical science in this chapter. The first is the Word of Wisdom and whether it conflicts or corroborates what we know about healthy dietary practices today. The second concerns the potentially contentious intersection between medicine and miracles. The third deals directly with the use of medical technologies and circumventing God's will.

The Word of Wisdom, Scientific Evidence, and Human Health

We'll keep this section short since most of us are keenly aware of the benefits of the Word of Wisdom. Our bodies are the pinnacle of God's Creation, created in His image (Genesis 1:27). *The Family: A Proclamation to the World* teaches that our physical bodies are essential to "gain earthly experience to progress toward perfection and ultimately realize [our] divine destiny as heirs of eternal life."[4] Thus, we are responsible for caring for our bodies and ensuring they are worthy vessels for our spirits. The Lord has given us guidance for maintaining a healthy body, and medical research backs it up.

There is a straightforward correlation between health and the guidelines in the Word of Wisdom. Fiber comes from consumption of plant materials (Doctrine and Covenants 89:10, 14). Repeated studies continue to show that diets high in fiber and low in fat and refined sugars promote health.[5] In addition, multiple studies have shown that natural sugars from fruit are far better than refined sugars (Doctrine and Covenants 89:11).[6] Lastly, research shows that the primary source of unhealthy fats in the diet comes from animal products, especially red meat,[7] something the Word of Wisdom cautions us to eat sparingly (Doctrine and Covenants 89:12). In short, research focused on healthy diets is consistent with the counsel in the Word of Wisdom.

The Word of Wisdom also prohibits alcohol consumption (Doctrine and Covenants 89:5). Research over the past several decades has warned against overuse of alcohol but has repeatedly found some health-protective benefits of small amounts of alcohol consumption[8]—you've probably heard some say that a glass of red wine a day is healthy. However, more recent research has confirmed that strict prohibition is a healthier alternative. A recent global study of 195 countries and 28 million individuals, looking at overall health consequences of alcohol consumption, solidly concluded that "the level of alcohol consumption that minimizes harm across health outcomes was zero."[9] It turns out that the modest health-protective benefits of moderate alcohol consumption are far outweighed by its harms to other health outcomes.

The research on the health effects of coffee and tea (those

specified as "hot drinks" [Doctrine and Covenants 89:9] as interpreted by the current *General Handbook*[10]) is still mixed.[11] Both are addictive. Some research has shown that drinking hot beverages, like coffee or tea, can increase the risk of esophageal cancer.[12] Recently, caffeine was shown to profoundly interrupt healthy sleep patterns, even if it is consumed early in the day.[13] So that's a start (although we should be clear that the Word of Wisdom does not prohibit other hot drinks, like hot cocoa, or other caffeinated drinks like some sodas). Tobacco is strictly prohibited by the Word of Wisdom (Doctrine and Covenants 89:8) and is the leading cause of preventable death in the United States[14] and likely the world.

When the Word of Wisdom was revealed to the Prophet Joseph Smith, the health reforms it suggested were still being hotly debated in society.[15] It has only been in the following decades that we have more fully understood the wisdom of obedience to its principles. Importantly, however, current harmony between medical discoveries and the Word of Wisdom is not the reason to live by God's dietary laws. God has given commandments about health practices that sometimes seem unusual or arbitrary. For example, Lehi's family was prohibited from lighting fires to cook their meat in the wilderness (1 Nephi 17:12). Through Moses the Lord gave strict commands for gathering manna that fell from heaven (Exodus 16:16–20). God's ways are not our ways (Isaiah 55:8). He may see problems of which we are not aware. When we follow His laws, we develop greater faith, and He is able to protect us and bless us.

Medicine and Miracles

Each of us, at some point, will find ourselves in need of healing from a physical ailment. There are two potential avenues for healing available. The first involves seeking the power of God on our behalf through prayer and priesthood authority. The second involves seeking medical attention. Both avenues are recommended by the Lord. President Dallin H. Oaks has assured us, "The use of medical science is not at odds with our prayers of faith and our reliance on priesthood blessings."[16]

Miracles can and do occur, but the Lord requires that we do all we can to prepare ourselves to receive such miracles.

Certainly modern medicine has yet to discover all potential remedies and treatments; we are not claiming that mainstream medicine is perfect. Modern medicine works best when patients are well-informed and proactive in finding information. A recent word of caution from the Church states: "We urge Church members to be cautious about participating in any group that promises—in exchange for money—miraculous healings or that claims to have special methods for accessing healing power outside of properly ordained priesthood holders."[17] We too caution readers to seek the counsel of wise medical experts.[18] In so doing, we can prepare ourselves in the most appropriate ways to receive a miracle.

Let us share a poignant story about how using faith and science together can bring about miracles, as told by Jamie:

> I was in the concluding semester of a graduate program and ecstatic to be having my first baby. All seemed routine until delivery when part of the placenta broke off, causing massive hemorrhaging. Thankfully, both my son and I survived the ordeal, although I could not stand or care for my son on my own for several weeks. Six weeks postpartum, I suffered another major hemorrhage and was rushed into emergency surgery. Thinking the hemorrhaging had been just an unfortunate fluke, we became pregnant again. This time, the danger of the situation presented itself early in the pregnancy, when, while fast asleep, I nearly bled to death in my bed. After a harrowing drive to the hospital, we were overjoyed to learn that the baby was still with us, but nervous to discover that the pregnancy would have intense complications. I had a badly misshapen placenta that covered the cervical opening (a life-threatening condition).
>
> After five long months of bed rest and several more scares, I delivered another healthy baby boy, but I nearly lost my life in the process (once again almost bleeding to death during delivery). Shortly after, I was diagnosed with a rare condition called Asherman's syndrome. Most women with

> this condition struggle to have any children at all, and those who do often suffer life-threatening complications like I did. This was devastating news, since I felt sure that my family was supposed to be larger. Certainly, I was grateful for my two beautiful sons, but I prayed every day for a miracle.
>
> But I didn't just sit back and pray, hoping that the Lord would step in and miraculously heal me. I believed that He would, and I knew that He had the power to do so, but I also did everything in *my* power to bring that miracle to pass. I consulted scientists and medical practitioners, researched the condition and possible treatments, and subjected myself to painful surgeries. Over the next seven years, I was blessed with two more sons (yes, I have four fabulous boys that I wouldn't trade for the world!). I do believe that the Lord blessed me with a miracle, and I believe that miracle was brought about by the power of God. I also believe that God used specialized scientific knowledge and the skillful hands of surgeons to do it. For me, bringing science and my faith together has blessed my life.

So what is a miracle? One source defines a miracle as "a beneficial event brought about through divine power that mortals do not understand."[19] Notice it does not say that a miracle is something that takes place without any possible physical explanation; it just says that we, as mortals, do not understand the process. Our Church teaches that "miracles cannot be in contravention of natural law, but are wrought through the operation of laws not universally or commonly recognized. . . . In the contemplation of the miracles wrought by Christ, we must of necessity recognize the operation of a power transcending our *present* human understanding."[20] Remember back to chapter 3 and the mistake of believing in a "God of the Gaps," which requires that miracles cannot be explained by science. Perhaps a better way to view miracles is to believe that God has knowledge of all the laws of the universe, many of which modern science has yet to discover. Thus, He can bring about miracles in ways that seem miraculous to you and me but which still obey natural laws that someday we may better understand.

And won't it be exciting to learn how God parted the Red Sea for the children of Israel (Exodus 14:21)? Or how He fed five thousand with five loaves of bread (Mark 6:41–44)? Or how He raised Lazarus from the dead (John 11:44)? His methods were not magical, nor did they defy logic, but the genius of His process will nonetheless cause us to marvel.

Do Medical Technologies Circumvent God's Will?

Now let's talk about some medical treatments and advances that tend to provoke controversy. Some are controversial due to the propagation of misinformation and pseudoscience that confuse the issue and leave many people unable to make an informed decision. Other medical practices are controversial on ethical grounds—those who use them are sometimes accused of "playing God." We'd like to tackle one issue that is controversial because of misinformation (vaccines) and two that are controversial due to ethical issues (reproductive technologies and genetic modification).

Vaccines

Vaccines are one of the most transformative advancements in the history of modern medicine, saving countless lives from preventable deaths and alleviating tremendous amounts of unnecessary suffering. Discovered in part by a physician named Edward Jenner,[21] the idea of inoculation is that if you expose your body to a pathogen (anything that causes disease, such as a virus or bacterium) that is similar enough to the "real thing," your body will build immunity to the disease. The process is somewhat complicated,[22] but suffice it to say, Jenner realized that cowpox (a mild form of smallpox in cattle) was close enough to the smallpox virus that if you caught it, you would be immune to smallpox, without having to actually catch it. Thus, the "vaccination" (*vacca* means cow) was born. Today, we have a variety of methods for promoting immunity through vaccination.[23] The type of vaccine produced often depends on the type of pathogen and severity of infection. But all vaccines go through rigorous testing during their development to make sure they are safe and effective. And we want to be very clear on one point—vaccines do not change or manipulate your DNA (some viruses, on the other hand, can!). They are simply designed to have the same effect on your immune system as catching the real disease would, without having to suffer the consequences of actual infection.

If vaccines are such a medical miracle, why is there so much controversy surrounding them? We covered part of the reason in chapter 4; much misinformation has been spread about vaccines for nefarious purposes. But like any medical advancement, a certain amount of trial and error has taken place in developing vaccines and refining safety protocols, and this has led to understandable skepticism; however, each case has led to better safety protocols and more regulation designed to keep us safe.[24] For example, in 1955, Cutter Laboratories produced a batch of vaccines intended to have attenuated polio virus, but due to a manufacturing error, the vaccines contained live virus. It resulted in 40,000 cases of polio, 164 cases of paralysis, and 10 deaths.[25] This led to much more stringent safety regulations.[26] In 1976, a batch of the flu vaccine resulted in abnormally high instances of Guillain-Barré syndrome (1 per 100,000,[27] with 53 deaths[28]), and more safety monitoring for influenza vaccines was instituted as a result. In a recent review of all deaths recorded in association with vaccines since recording began, researchers found conclusive linkage between vaccines and less than 15 deaths in four categories: in cases where individuals had a severe anaphylactic reaction to an ingredient, in cases where a live attenuated vaccine was given to someone with a severely weakened immune system, in cases where patients had a rare nonallergic interaction with the vaccine, and in cases where patients died from fainting and hitting their heads after receiving a vaccine.[29]

What have our Church leaders said about vaccines? Most recently, in the midst of the COVID-19 pandemic, the First Presidency issued this statement: "As appropriate opportunities become available, the Church urges its members, employees and missionaries to be good global citizens and help quell the pandemic by safeguarding themselves and others through immunization." They went on to emphasize, "In word and deed, The Church of Jesus Christ of Latter-day Saints has supported vaccinations for generations."[30] In 1978, the First Presidency stated, "We urge members of The Church of Jesus Christ of Latter-day Saints to protect their own children through immunization."[31] In fact, Church humanitarian efforts have funded 168 projects in 46 countries to provide life-saving immunizations to bless more than 116,819,870 people.[32] The Church has always had a positive stance toward the life-saving science of vaccination. This does not mean that we need to accept vaccines blindly or that we can't ask questions or seek reputable answers concerning vaccine safety for our own individual circumstances. But we can have similar confidence that just as the Word of Wisdom betters our lives, the prophetic recommendation of vaccinations will as well.

Reproductive Technologies

As part of their covenants with God, married couples have been commanded to "multiply and replenish the Earth."[33] There is perhaps no greater calling than being a parent. However, the decision to have children may not be under our immediate control. In some cases, due to genetic or anatomical abnormalities or other circumstances, we may be unable to conceive or produce a viable child without medical intervention. The *General Handbook* states, "When needed, reproductive technology can assist a married woman and man in their righteous desire to have children. This technology includes artificial insemination and in vitro fertilization."[34]

Artificial insemination is the medical insertion of sperm to increase the odds of pregnancy. While the Church discourages "using sperm from anyone but the husband or an egg from anyone but the wife," the ultimate decision is left to the married couple.[35] Is using artificial means to facilitate conception somehow undermining God's will? One way to look at this decision is to consider what the purpose of conception is. It is to provide bodies for God's spirit children.[36] If reproductive technology can help meet our greatest calling, then it may be considered a gift from God.

In vitro fertilization is the forming of an embryo outside the body by combining an egg from the mother and a sperm from the father in a laboratory and then placing the fertilized egg into the uterus. For example, let's say that Peter and Susan want to have a baby, but they know that they are both carriers of a rare recessive genetic disease that, if inherited, will cause the fetus to die prior to birth. That means by chance alone, 25% of their children will die in utero. That doesn't mean that they are guaranteed three healthy babies for every one loss. (We knew a couple in this situation that lost two out of their three children; probability is not always fair.)

Peter and Susan can take their chances naturally and risk possibly losing child after child. Alternatively, they may try in vitro fertilization. In this case, doctors would take multiple eggs from Susan and fertilize them with Peter's sperm. They would let the embryos go through a few cell divisions before safely pulling one cell from the mass that is the embryo and performing genetic testing on it to ensure that the embryo is healthy before it is implanted. The ethical dilemma comes if the embryo is not healthy. What if it has the disease? Or what if you get more healthy embryos than you can safely implant? Do you discard them? Many people choose not to do in vitro fertilization for this reason. The Church does not have specific guidance for these scenarios, so, once again, the decision is left up to the couple and the Lord. We can offer a statistical way of looking at this scenario. We will spare you the math, but for Peter and Susan the chance of losing a child before birth is nearly five times higher than the risk of losing an embryo through in vitro. We want to be clear that we are not arguing for or against in vitro, but there may be situations, such as this one, in which a couple may want to prayerfully consider it as an option.

Genetic Modification

What if we could intentionally manipulate the DNA of Peter and Susan's embryo to change its genetics, thus saving the baby's life and eliminating the need to discard any embryos? As medical technology advances, this is becoming more of a reality. This is a recent medical breakthrough, and the Church has given no specific direction on genetic modification. All we can offer is that the Church has consistently looked favorably upon medical advancements that improve or prolong life: "Latter-day Saints believe in applying the best available scientific knowledge and techniques. We use nutrition, exercise, and other practices to preserve health, and we enlist the help of healing practitioners, such as physicians and surgeons, to restore health."[37] Do these technologies fit this purview to preserve and restore health? Perhaps. Is there the potential for these procedures to cross an ethical boundary? Possibly. But with an eye turned toward the gospel, we can navigate these exciting avenues ahead.

Let us share one real scenario with you. Spinal muscular atrophy (SMA) is a devastating genetic disease that causes muscles to waste away and, in its most common form, leads to death in early childhood.[38] SMA affects between 5 and 25 out of 100,000 children,[39] making it one of the leading genetic causes of infant death.[40] The most common form results from a genetic defect in one gene that is inherited from both parents who are carriers. Just like Peter and Susan, parents who are both carriers have a 25% chance of passing the disease on to their children, with devastating results. Recent advancements in gene therapy, however, have made it possible to correct the mutation in the child, effectively reversing the effects of SMA.[41] It is a complicated procedure, but in basic terms, it involves introducing the correct DNA into the child (using a virus), thus replacing the mutation that leads to death.

In this case, is it okay to manipulate a child's DNA in order to save them from suffering and death? (Affected babies usually die of respiratory failure, their breathing muscles becoming too weak to allow them to take a breath.) Or is it best to allow that spirit to obtain a body and then quickly return to their Father in Heaven, having briefly passed through mortality? We know that "all children who die before they arrive at the years of accountability are saved in the celestial kingdom of heaven" (Doctrine and Covenants 137:10) and that one of the main purposes of mortality is simply to receive a body. Elder Bruce R. McConkie remarked, at the death of his infant granddaughter, "There are certain spirits who come into this life only to receive bodies; for reasons that we do not know, but which are known in the infinite wisdom of the Eternal Father, they do not need the testing, probationary experience of mortality."[42] Maybe this is all that these children need. Perhaps, however, these children have things to learn here in mortality; perhaps they need the chance to "prove [themselves], choose to come unto Christ, and prepare to be worthy of eternal life."[43] Perhaps the Lord has given us this knowledge to prolong their life and give them the opportunities the Lord intended for them to have. This reasoning may apply to medical procedures to prolong the life of adults as well (for example, cancer treatments, organ transplants, and life-saving surgeries). There is not one right answer to these questions. Of course, there are also lots of potential genetic modifications that do not prolong life but would perhaps increase the quality of life. Again, we can't offer a definitive answer. The goal of medical technology is not to supersede God's will. It only allows us the opportunity to accept God's will. One can pray earnestly and seek the Lord's counsel, and with faith, the Lord will reveal His will to those who seek it.

Conclusion

In an era when human knowledge and medical technologies are advancing at an unprecedented rate, it is good to keep our eyes firmly focused on the principles of the gospel and the purpose of mortality in the great plan of happiness. Combining the possibilities brought about through medical technology with fervent prayer and consultation with priesthood authority, we can receive health and vigor that will allow us to realize some of the deepest and long-lasting blessings this life has to offer.

CHAPTER 8

NATURE VERSUS NURTURE

The debate over "nature" versus "nurture" has been ongoing since at least the discovery of genetic inheritance in the late 1800s.[1] How much of who we are is determined by our inherited genes? And how does this affect our pursuit of exaltation and eternal life? This is a topic that can at least be partially addressed by science and enlightened by religious understanding.

Our physical bodies provide our spirits with incredible abilities to accomplish things that we could never do without a body.[2] One of the great blessings of choosing the Lord's plan is that we get to come down to earth and receive our physical bodies. Our bodies, however, are mortal and subject to mortal laws; they have variations, sometimes flaws, and often challenges that cause us to hurt, to suffer, and to question, but also to learn, to refine ourselves, and to become more like the people we want to be in the eternities. This is also a part of Heavenly Father's plan. We have been given agency, and with that agency, we are also given challenges and choices. As Elder D. Todd Christofferson explains, "The gift of agency is intended to give us experience. We 'taste the bitter, that [we] may know to prize the good' (Moses 6:55)."[3]

Each of us is unique because we are individual spirit children of God who existed prior to this earth *and* because we inhabit a genetically unique mortal body built by a mortal mother with genetic directions provided from both of our mortal parents. In addition, each of us is exposed to different environments, experiences, and trials throughout mortality. We receive different blessings and opportunities. We make different choices using our God-given agency. All of these elements combine to make each of our mortal journeys unique. It is no wonder that God is the only one who can truly know us.

Some of these mortal characteristics cause significant challenges to our spirits and require us to put all our faith in God's grace and plan. As the Lord tells us, "I give unto men weakness that they may be humble; and my grace is sufficient for all men that humble themselves before me; for if they humble themselves before me, and have faith in me, then will I make weak things become strong unto them" (Ether 12:27). Our challenge is to "[put] off the natural man and [become] a saint through the atonement of Christ the Lord" (Mosiah 3:19).

What about Nature and Nurture Needs Reconciliation?

In this chapter we are going to talk about traits. Traits are defined as "any observable characteristic at any level of observation of an individual."[4] Some of our traits give us perceived advantages in some situations, like a musical trait that allows a composer to write beautiful symphonies, or a compassionate trait that allows a humanitarian to be completely selfless in pursuing the greater good. Other traits give us perceived disadvantages in some situations, like dyslexia that can make reading and learning difficult, or extreme introversion that causes even minute social interactions to be debilitating. These are all traits that make us who we are and shape our mortal experiences.

The questions that then arise are to what extent are our traits controlled by genetics (by our mortal architecture—that is, "nature"); to what extent are they controlled by our environment (that is, "nurture"); and what do we control through our agency? We will address these questions through both a scientific and spiritual lens. Then we will address how our physical bodies interact with our spiritual nature and how this interaction leads to a poignant question: how can we possibly judge one another?

How Much Is Controlled by
"Nature" versus "Nurture"?

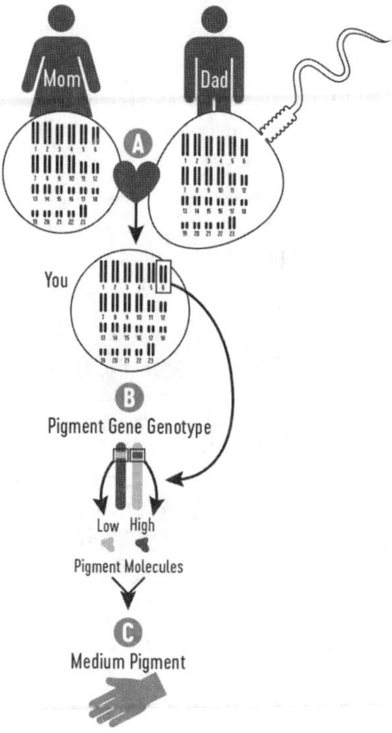

Figure 8.1. Genetics Overview

Let's explore how science can help us understand how our physical bodies influence our traits. To understand this, we need a brief background in genetics. All the instructions required to build our body—every protein, tissue, and cell—is contained in the 46 chromosomes that we inherit from our parents (see figure 8.1A). Chromosomes consist of long strands of DNA (deoxyribonucleic acid), segments of which are called "genes" (see figure 8.1B); each gene codes for a protein that does a specific job or task in our body (for example, our skin is made of collagen proteins, our heart has actin and myosin proteins, our blood cells are made up of hemoglobin proteins, and so on). Our 46 chromosomes actually consist of two nearly identical sets (23 from our mom and 23 from our dad); they contain the same genes in the same order, but can differ slightly in the recipes—for an over-simplified example, let's say the gene for a particular skin pigment on our dad's chromosome[5] might code for high levels, but our mom's might code for very little pigment (see figure 8.1B). When our skin cells make pigment, they assess both genes and combine the results, so in this particular case, the result would be a medium level of pigment (see figure 8.1C). Some traits are controlled by just one gene (like earlobe shape or widow's peak), but most (including skin color from our example) are controlled by a complex combination of genes, involving the addition of each pair of recipes into the final product: you. This is what we mean when we refer to your "genotype" or your "genetics." Your genetics consist of the unique combination of recipes that you received from your parents.

Our genetics tell our body what to make, but there are also controls that determine *when* to make something and *how much* of it to make. These controls can be influenced by the environment. For example, when stressed, our bodies overproduce the protein cortisol.[6] In excess, cortisol can suppress the immune system and contribute to psychological and physical disorders (such as obesity).[7] The outside environment's control of the expression of our genes is referred to as gene-environment interactions or gene regulation. Additionally, there are controls that can affect chromosome structure and turn genes "on" or "off," referred to as *epigenetics*.[8] Together, the combination of genetics and environmental interactions create a range of possible physical outcomes.[9] This means that, hypothetically, if you had two people who were absolutely identical in their genetics and you exposed them to two different environments, they may look, act, and feel differently. This plays a large role in the nature-nurture conversation. Our nature (our genetics) provides the baseline for that range of possibilities; in other words, we can produce only the physical outcomes for which we have the genetic recipes. But our nurture (our environment) plays upon our nature to determine where on that range we fall.

Here is a simple example of the interplay between genes and environment: If a person inherits two copies of a faulty breast cancer gene (BRCA1 or BRCA2), they are much more likely to develop breast cancer.[10] However, environmental factors largely determine whether they *will* develop cancer (for example, whether they smoke or drink, how much they exercise, or environmental hazards to which they have been exposed). This same principle can be applied to all traits with a genetic basis, including behavioral traits.

When we are dealing with very complex traits like behavior, personality, talents, or mental states, it is difficult to determine which exact genes are involved because there are many genes and because of the heavy influence of environment. To try to determine how much of these traits come from our genes, scientists calculate a "heritability index." Before the advent of DNA-sequencing technology, a common way to do this was to use twins. Identical twins[11] have almost no differences in their DNA; fraternal twins[12] share about 50% of their DNA, on average. So if a particular trait is more similar in identical twins than in fraternal twins, given that they are raised in the same environment, then genetics likely play a larger role. Additionally, if twins are separated at birth and raised in different environments but share more traits than would be expected between complete strangers, again, a higher genetic influence would be suspected.[13] With new DNA technologies, scientists can run what are called genome-wide association studies (GWAS), in which they actually sequence the DNA of individuals with and without a particular trait to determine if there are certain genes that are more commonly found in those with the trait.

It is critical, however, to distinguish between *heritability* and *heritable*. When we say something is *heritable*—that is, we inherited it directly from our parents—we are talking about only the genetics we received and their direct influence on our traits.

Heritability, on the other hand, differs in two important ways: First, it is looking at population-level (*not* individual-level) variation in a trait, so you cannot assign this value directly to an individual. (If, for example, musical ability has a heritability index of 0.2, we cannot say that 20% of Joe's musical talent came directly from his parents through genetics. Instead, we can only say that on average, in a population, 20% of the variation we see in musical talent is likely explained by inherited genetics from parents.) Second, heritability includes *all* the many factors that will influence that variability, including genetics, but also including environment.[14] We will emphasize again: complex traits are just that—complex.

In the field of behavioral genetics, scientists have looked at a number of human traits that they classify as behavioral, meaning they influence the way a person will act, feel, interact with others and the environment, or even think. (At this point, we are examining strictly biological principles and are leaving out our ability to choose, for the moment.) These traits include intellectual ability, personality, mental health, self-confidence, sense of identity, and more. Contrast this with the more colloquial use of "behavior," often referenced when speaking of children throwing tantrums or teenagers being rebellious; this usage refers only to choice. When it comes to human behavioral traits, scientific studies have repeatedly and robustly shown that their heritability is extremely large, typically between 30% and 50%. (Compare this to other psychological differences that have been studied, like differences between male and female behaviors, where heritability has been found to be less than 1%).[15] But this also likely means that the remaining 50% to 70% of the variation in human behaviors can be attributed to environment (nurture).

To illustrate these biological principles, we have chosen three human behavioral traits to examine more closely: mental health, addiction, and gender identity (all three of these traits are considered "behavioral" traits by scientists using the definition above). We will first outline what we know from a scientific perspective, then talk about how to reconcile this knowledge with our religious understanding.

Mental Health

When we talk about mental health, let's specifically address what are called psychopathologies (*psycho-* means mind, and *patholog-* means disease), which include depression, anxiety, attention deficit disorder, bipolar disorder, obsessive-compulsive disorder, autism, and many more. Elder Jeffrey R. Holland taught, "[Mental health] afflictions are some of the realities of mortal life, and there should be no more shame in acknowledging them than in acknowledging a battle with high blood pressure or the sudden appearance of a malignant tumor."[16] Mental health traits are every bit as influenced by physiological malfunctions as diabetes or Parkinson's disease are (in other words, classifying these traits as a "behavior," as scientists do, does not imply that they are only a choice). Seeking treatment for them is every bit as logical as taking high blood pressure medicine or insulin injections. We would not expect someone with a broken arm to just "suck it up and put on a happy face," nor can we expect that of someone with clinical depression or obsessive-compulsive disorder, for example.

The science is pretty clear that psychopathologies are highly influenced by our genetics. Research has established that major depressive disorders,[17] generalized anxiety disorders,[18] schizophrenia,[19] autism spectrum disorders,[20] obsessive-compulsive disorders,[21] and more[22] have high heritability. This means that, after controlling for environmental factors (home environment, childhood experiences, nutrition, education, choices, and so on), genetics still can significantly predict these disorders, accounting for 30% to 50% of the variation we see in the population.[23] This percentage is very significant for genetically influenced traits. Most of these disorders are controlled by many different genes working in concert, however, so we cannot simply identify one gene and then predict whether someone will have the disorder. Consider also that each of these genes are also influenced by the environment. Figuring out the exact genetic mechanisms quickly becomes complicated and is often out of reach for current science. These conditions, however, are no less heritable or real.

Addiction

As we talk of addiction here, we will specifically cover the research concerning abuse of substances, including alcohol, nicotine, illicit drugs, and so on. (This discussion could also apply to other addictions such as to pornography or video games; we are just not highlighting that research here.) The Lord has given prudent advice to His prophets that can save us from much suffering (see Doctrine and Covenants 89). We know that addictive substances work on brain neuroreceptors in ways that *cause* addiction.[24] Research has even shown that these substances can permanently change our brain function, our behavior, and ultimately our quality of life.[25] However, have you wondered why some people can indulge once in a potentially harmful substance and then easily turn away, while others are hooked for life? As it turns out, it has to do with our genetics.

Congruent with the psychopathology research discussed above, studies have repeatedly and consistently shown a strong heritability of addictive behaviors.[26] Not only do we have broad-scale genomic studies indicating genetic influence, but in the case of addiction, scientists have also identified specific genes that increase the risk of dependence and that work in a similar fashion to the breast cancer gene discussed earlier. For example, particular mutations in neuronal genes (neuronal nicotinic acetylcholine receptors or nAChRs) can increase both your vulnerability to tobacco dependence and your risk for lung cancer.[27] For alcoholism, we have identified both protective and high-risk genes: A mutation in one gene causes alcohol-induced flushing, low blood pressure, a fast heart rate, dizziness, anxiety, nausea, headaches, and weakness, making these individuals far *less* likely to consume alcohol or become dependent;[28] on the other hand, variations in a gene that breaks down alcohol can *increase* your risk of alcoholism.[29] A host of other genes have been identified that relate to one's response to treatment for alcoholism (meaning that treatments will have different success rates on different people, based on their genetics).[30] While we have not identified specific genes that lead to other addictions (for example, pornography), research suggests that similar genetic influences may be at play.[31] And while we have a good idea of genetic influences on addictive behaviors, like all personality traits, substance addiction is likely a result of a combination of genes coupled with environmental influence and choice.

Biological Sex, Sexual Orientation, and Gender Identity

Before we begin our discussion of the science related to biological sex and gender identity, we want to be clear that God loves all His children. Our discussion here is of necessity brief, and the data we cite should not be weaponized. The traits surrounding gender and sex are incredibly complex, and the lack of adequate long-term research, and the individual nature of each person's situation suggest a need for great compassion for transgender individuals, as well as others within the LGBTQ community, especially as they seek to establish faith within the Church of Jesus Christ. Elder Quentin L. Cook offers excellent counsel as we seek to include individuals who identify as LGBTQ: "As a church, nobody should be more loving and compassionate. Let us be at the forefront in terms of expressing love, compassion, and outreach. Let's not have families exclude or be disrespectful of those who choose a different lifestyle as a result of their feelings about their own gender."[32] An open dialogue with both the science and the revealed truth on this topic can foster mutual love and respect as we continue to navigate this complicated issue.

Biological Sex

We'll start with biological sex from a direct, purely scientific perspective. In humans, sex determination is fairly straightforward (unlike some other organisms, like certain reptiles, where variations in temperature can alter the sex of the offspring[33]). And we'll view it at four stages: chromosomes at conception, embryonic development, sex at birth, and puberty. At conception, our 23rd pair of chromosomes determines our sex: males receive a Y and females receive an X chromosome from their father (the mother always donates an X chromosome, so males are XY and females are XX). Once the sperm and egg come together, embryonic development begins. The initial embryo has an undetermined sex and actually possesses primitive structures of both the male and female reproductive tracts. The main reason that receiving a Y chromosome turns a fetus into a male is due to the activation of a very specific gene on that chromosome called the "sex-determining region Y protein," or *SRY*, along with a few associated genes.[34] Usually when this gene is both present and active, it turns on a set of genes that will ultimately turn the sex organs into the vas deferens, epididymis, and penis, and the gonads into testicles (*gonads* is the generic term for the organs that produce reproductive cells: testes and ovaries). If you do not have a Y chromosome, the sex organs will eventually differentiate into a uterus, fallopian tubes, vagina, and clitoris, and the gonads into ovaries. If all the cascades occur typically, the newborn will have external genitalia that match the internal reproductive structures and the chromosomal configuration (XX or XY). Thus, at birth, in most cases, the sex can be determined accurately.

An additional way to look at biological sex is to determine the size of the gametes (*gamete* is the generic term for sex cells) produced by the gonads. Biologically, in almost all sexually reproducing organisms, we define the *male* as the one that produces the small gametes (for example, sperm and pollen grains) and the *female* as the one that produces the large gametes (for example, eggs).[35]

Lastly, many of the features associated with biological sex are secondary sexual characteristics (for example, the development of breasts, the pitch of our voice, the shape of our hips and shoulders, the places we grow hair, sexual behavior, and so on) and they don't develop until puberty. These are tightly controlled by our genes (for example, through hormone production and regulation), and these genes are controlled by biological sex. But, just like other genetic characteristics, environmental interactions and epigenetic controls combined with multiple gene interactions lead to a range of physical and behavioral characteristics—that is, the environment can play a large role in the development and physical outcomes of these secondary sexual characteristics.[36] In short, most of us have seen variations in "masculinity" and "femininity" among our friends, family, and acquaintances.

Variations in Development

What we described above was the typical developmental process. Let's discuss, for just a moment, some of the variations that can occur. At conception, it is possible to inherit a third sex chromosome and be XXX, XXY, or XYY (this is a "trisomy," similar to trisomy 21, which causes Down syndrome) or inherit only one X chromosome (a single Y chromosome leads to miscarriage).[37] These conditions often come with a host of detrimental side effects, although sometimes a person may not even be aware of the chromosomal abnormality.[38] In most cases, if the SRY gene is active, embryonic development proceeds normally and biological sex is obvious at birth.

Some may wonder if a person can receive a Y chromosome but have an inactive SRY gene and, therefore, not have the associated cascade of activity, and appear as a female. This is possible, but rare.[39] Other mutations in the host of cascade proteins can also cause a mismatch of external and internal sexual structures and/or chromosomes, making sex determination at birth more ambiguous and possibly causing secondary sexual characteristics to also be mismatched.[40]

Sexual Orientation

One of the secondary sexual characteristics that develops around puberty is one's sexual attraction or sexual orientation. From a biological perspective, heterosexual individuals are attracted to the opposite biological sex from their own, whereas homosexual individuals are attracted to the same sex. (This is different from gender identity, which we will discuss in a moment.) One question might be, are those who are LGBT+[41] genetically different from those who are not? First, let's look at the heritability of LGB traits (the research here addresses only those who are lesbian, gay, or bisexual) and then explore if there are any specific genes that would suggest a genetic component. In twin studies (and we note these studies are small and not well replicated[42]), concordance in same-sex sexual behaviors between twins suggested potential heritability around 37% in males and 18% in females.[43] That there are differences in heritability between sexes suggests that the inheritance of sexual preference goes beyond simple genetics (genes that would be expected to influence the two sexes equally) and that hormonal and social influences may play a role. Recently, in a large-scale genome-wide association study, population-level comparisons suggested an upward limit of 8% to 25% heritability.[44] Remember that heritability is not the same as "inherited" for two reasons: first, it works at the population level, and, second, it measures both genetic and epigenetic factors without disentangling them. When looking strictly at genetic influence on an individual, scientists have estimated that genetics explains less than 1% of the trait, meaning that, at present, the genetic information we have cannot predict if a person will be gay or bisexual.[45] Researchers have come to understand that sexual orientation is likely controlled by multiple genes, along with a large environmental (possibly including a social) influence.[46] To date, science has not uncovered any one gene that can predict sexual orientation. Sexuality is much more complex than that.

Gender Identity

Gender identity, as opposed to the more scientific concept of biological sex, has been defined as an individual's self-conception of their gender.[47] In this definition, gender identity is a psychosocial, rather than strictly biological, trait. The development of matching internal and external sex organs as well as secondary sexual characteristics can play a role in how one might identify. Regarding chromosomal anomalies, the trisomies of the sex chromosomes (XXX, XXY, XYY, and XO) are not equivalent to the *intersex* term being used today, which is a much larger umbrella term that encompasses any number of anatomical and even nonanatomical anomalies that cause a person to have a less-obvious gender or gender identity. Having an extra sex chromosome also does not seem to increase one's chances of being or identifying as gay or intersex.[48]

Gender diversity (for example, transgender individuals) is currently harder to define genetically. Some have suggested that individuals are born transgender—that it is genetic. Here is what we presently know from the current body of research: Most children who are gender diverse are unlikely to identify as transgender in adulthood if parents and clinicians engage in "watchful waiting," characterized by patiently seeking to help these children feel comfortable with their birth sex until they go through puberty.[49] Puberty generally brings resolution for these children, and it does not appear to be a genetically predetermined condition. Regarding adults who transition to a different gender through sex-reassignment surgery, the follow-up studies that have been done have been unable to keep most respondents enrolled for the full length of the studies, making the data unclear,[50] and data are just beginning to be gathered on nonsurgical transitions and hormone therapies. There is current debate within the medical community as to the standard of care for transgender individuals.[51]

We realize that this is a sensitive issue, and although we have presented information in a straightforward way, we hope that compassion comes through in our writing. This is one matter for which both our scientific and our religious knowledge may currently be incomplete, and we may have to live with a degree of uncertainty (as we discussed in chapter 5, comfort with uncertainty is key in reconciling science and religion). In 2015, President Dallin H. Oaks said in an interview, "Being acquainted with the unique problems of a transgender situation is something we have not had so much experience with, and we have some unfinished business in teaching on that."[52] We do know that the Church teaches that "gender is an essential characteristic of individual premortal, mortal, and eternal identity and purpose."[53] President Oaks further clarified that "the intended meaning of gender . . . as used in Church statements and publications . . . is biological sex at birth."[54]

In regard to identity, President Russell M. Nelson taught the youth of the Church: "Who are you? First and foremost, you are a child of God. Second, as a member of the Church, you are a child of the covenant. And third, you are a disciple of Jesus Christ. . . . I plead with you not to replace these three paramount and unchanging identifiers with any others, because doing so could stymie your progress or pigeonhole you in a stereotype that could potentially thwart your eternal progression."[55] Thus, from our prophets we learn that our primary and eternal identity is a child of God, a child of the covenant, and a disciple of Jesus Christ.

This, though, does not discount the importance of secondary identities to our mental health, well-being, or sense of self. Secondary identities, such as "mother," "athlete," "extrovert," or "gay" can play important roles in who we are. Elder D. Todd Christofferson reminded us that sexual orientation "is but one aspect of any person's life and it need not become the consuming aspect of his or her life." Importantly, he continues, "One thing that is always important is to recognize the feelings of a person, that they are real. That they are authentic. That we don't deny that someone feels a certain way. . . . I believe it is crucial that we always continue to feel that, to express that, to acknowledge the reality of people's feelings and circumstances and go from there."[56] May we approach those who identify differently than we do with respect and compassion.

How Does Our Physical Body Interact with Our Spiritual Nature?

We hope it is clear from the scientific literature reviewed above that human traits are highly complex. Some traits have significant genetic ties, and most traits have substantial environmental influence as well. So how do these findings relate to our belief that our bodies are the physical house for our spirits? Let's revisit why we are here. We chose to follow Christ and to come to earth to receive a physical body. This body allows us to experience things that our spirits could not do without it. It allows us to develop our talents, to serve others, to build the kingdom, to understand joy and sorrow, pleasure and pain, success and failure. And through these experiences, we learn and we grow to become more like our Heavenly Parents. Our bodies are also mortal, and with that mortality comes strengths and weaknesses in some areas, temptations and triumphs in others. And because each of our bodies is genetically unique, and the environments in which our genes are expressed are unique, our experiences are also unique. Where one person suffers from clinical depression, another person might have uncommon optimism. Where another person may be inordinately challenged by addictive substances, another person might have uncanny willpower and self-control. And where one person might develop same-sex attraction, another might develop completely in-line with heterosexuality.

None of us has been endowed with a perfect body. Each of us is a unique spirit that requires unique experiences to achieve the right refinement. In God's infinite wisdom, He has provided us with a body fit for our exact needs required to teach us what we need to learn. Elder David A. Bednar taught, "In the classroom of mortality, we experience tenderness, love, kindness, happiness, sorrow, disappointment, pain, and even the challenges of physical limitations in ways that prepare us for eternity. Simply stated, there are lessons we must learn and experiences we must have, as the scriptures describe, 'according to the flesh' (1 Nephi 19:6; Alma 7:12–13)."[57]

Through our strengths, we can bless the lives of those around us and make relatively easy progress toward eternal life. Through our weaknesses, we can refine our spirits and learn the mortal lessons intended for us. The requirement for overcoming our weaknesses is simply applying Christ's Atonement until we come into complete harmony with the laws and ordinances of the gospel. President Thomas S. Monson declared, "The spiritual nature within us should not be dominated by the physical. It behooves each of us to remember who he or she is and what God expects him or her to become."[58] We are profoundly grateful for the gift of mortality *and* for the atoning sacrifice of our Savior. Life is challenging. It is supposed to be. We are told that "it must needs be, that there is an opposition in all things. If not so, . . . righteousness could not be brought to pass, . . . neither good nor bad" (2 Nephi 2:11). Thus, it is up to us to "choose liberty and eternal life, . . . or to choose captivity and death" (2 Nephi 2:27). And regarding our bodies and our understanding of complex issues, we are promised that "if your eye be single to my glory, your whole bodies shall be filled with light, . . . and that body which is filled with light comprehendeth all things" (Doctrine and Covenants 88:67).

How Can We Judge?

This leads us to our last point; it is one we make frequently with our students. We have sometimes heard people comparing weaknesses as if we can rank them according to their difficulty to overcome. For example, one might claim that living with obsessive-compulsive disorder is harder than pushing forward in the midst of depression, or that overcoming desires to use alcohol is harder than overcoming a pornography addiction. The point of ranking them is often to justify our own actions or inactions. From a genetic, as well as a spiritual, perspective, this reasoning is deeply flawed.

First, from a biological perspective, we have just discussed the significant interactions of our genes and the environment in which we dwell and how this affects our traits. As a result, each of us has a very different "genetic palette" from which we paint our pictures. Thus, each of us will approach life differently. Given that most of our behaviors cannot be pinpointed to any one gene, it is impossible for *anyone* to know how "hard" or "easy" living with any biological trait might be . . . anyone, that is, except the Lord.

Second, from a spiritual perspective, we must acknowledge that we are agents unto ourselves (Doctrine and Covenants 29:39). God has asked "that every man may act in doctrine and principle . . . according to the moral agency which I have given unto him, that every man may be accountable for his own sins in the day of judgment" (Doctrine and Covenants

101:78). Elder D. Todd Christofferson explains that "using our agency to choose God's will, and not slackening even when the going gets hard, . . . will make us like Him. God gave us agency, and Jesus showed us how to use it so that we could eventually learn what They know, do what They do, and become what They are."[59] But, the *way* in which we use our agency is influenced by our mortal bodies. The Lord knows each of us intimately and individually (including our genetic predispositions and our environmental influences). He "seeth not as man seeth; for man looketh on the outward appearance, but the Lord looketh on the heart" (1 Samuel 16:7). The Lord knows our genetics, desires, thoughts, and intentions. That is why *only He* can judge fairly. Joseph Smith wisely taught, "But while one portion of the human race are judging and condemning the other without mercy, the great parent of the universe looks upon the whole of the human family with a fatherly care and paternal regard. . . . He holds the reins of judgment in his hands; he is a wise Lawgiver, and will judge all men, [not according to the narrow, contracted, notions of men]"—that is, "not according to what they have not, but what they have."[60]

We, as humans with diverse mortal traits, do not have the ability or capacity to judge others for their traits without the full knowledge of their circumstances, experiences, intentions, and capacities. Therefore, it is our role only to look upon each other with great compassion, to help each other along the covenant path, and to follow the counsel of Alma "to bear one another's burdens . . . to mourn with those that mourn; yea, and comfort those that stand in need of comfort" (Mosiah 18:8–9).

Conclusion

In this chapter we have discussed both the genetic and environmental influences on our traits. While we have agency to choose our actions, each person's mortal experience is uniquely shaped by their own genetics interacting with their spirits. Let us remember that only the Lord has perfect eyes to see past the different genetic predispositions we all possess and truly see our intentions.

CHAPTER 9

ENVIRONMENTAL STEWARDSHIP

It seems like everywhere you turn today there are messages about environmental destruction; predictions of global catastrophe, animal extinction, and irreversible climate degradation; and constant reminders of our role in destroying the planet. These messages can create feelings of despair, sadness, or helplessness but also sometimes annoyance, anger, dismissiveness, or defensiveness. We will take a different approach here. We would like to approach "Creation Care" (a term many Christian organizations have adopted[1]) from the viewpoint that we are stewards of God's creations. God has promised that there is enough with some to spare (Doctrine and Covenants 104:17) and that the earth is for the use of humans (Doctrine and Covenants 49:19–21) to bring to pass our immortality and eternal life (Moses 1:39). This is a message of hope that, as righteous stewards, we can improve our current condition. Regarding the earth, President Russell M. Nelson stated, "As beneficiaries of the divine Creation, what shall we do? We should care for the earth, be wise stewards over it, and preserve it for future generations."[2] Environmental stewardship is a manifestation of our love for the Creator, each other, and our posterity.

What Aspects of Environmental Stewardship Need Reconciliation?

When it comes to environmental stewardship, there are three main issues that we'd like to discuss: What does it mean to be a "steward"? How do I differentiate between the data and someone's political or social "agenda"? And, given the data, do I really need to change my behaviors?

What Does It Mean to Be a Steward?

Let's start with what we know about the earth. We know that God created the earth and all things in it (Genesis 1:9, 11, 20–21; Moses 2:2, 9, 11, 20) and that God was pleased with His creations (Moses 2:12). The culmination of God's Creation was us—you and me—and He gave us "dominion" over all the earth and everything on it (Genesis 1:26; Moses 2:28). *Dominion* is an interesting word to use. In Hebrew, the word is *radah*, meaning "to rule." But the preposition *over* is not accurate; a more accurate translation might be "to exercise skilled mastery with respect to."[3] Out of curiosity, we asked our students to interpret the word *dominion* by asking, first, if they thought that humans were meant to "rule" over the rest of nature, and second, how they interpret "rule." We were surprised to find that nearly 60% of our students agreed with the use of "rule" and more than 85% defined rule as to "use for one's own benefit or to control," while less than 15% defined it in terms of "being mindful of" or "taking care of" the Lord's creations.[4] Clearly there are some misconceptions about what our role, as Latter-day Saints and stewards, is here on earth.

We are taught that all things on the earth were created for us to live in abundance (Doctrine and Covenants 49:19). We are also warned that we are accountable for our use of God's handiwork (Doctrine and Covenants 104:13–14). Let's replace the word *dominion* with *stewardship*. We are "stewards," not "owners."[5] There is a difference. What does it mean to be a "steward" of the blessings we have here on earth?

To be a steward means to be mindful of our resources and to respect the earth as a blessing from our Heavenly Father. We are taught that "it pleaseth God that he hath given all these things unto man; for unto this end were they made to be used," but the Lord goes on to explain that our use should be "with judgment, not to excess, neither by extortion" (Doctrine and Covenants 59:20). The earth was meant to be inhabited by God's children (1 Nephi 17:36), and we are asked to respect the earth as a gift from God. Elder Neal A. Maxwell remarked, "True disciples [of Christ] . . . would be consistent environmentalists—caring both about maintaining the spiritual health of a marriage and preserving a rainforest; caring about preserving the nutrient capacity of a family as well as providing a healthy supply of air and water."[6]

Second, to be a steward means to be accountable for our actions on the environment and to do our best to act wisely. Our stewardship is a sacred responsibility and should not be taken lightly. Bishop Gérald Caussé taught: "The care of the earth and of our natural environment is a sacred responsibility entrusted to us by God, which should fill us with a deep sense of duty and humility. It is also an integral component of our discipleship."[7] This means that doing our very best to become students of science in order to gain a sound understanding of the earth and its properties is a central part of our discipleship. To us, using both ways of knowing together—both science *and* religion—can help us accomplish what the Lord has asked.

How Do I Differentiate between the Data and an Agenda?

Few topics create more tension among friends and families than those that are politically charged, those that involve moral value judgments based on sound scientific evidence. Climate change tends to be one of those topics. In fact, according to recent data, political affiliation is the strongest predictor of one's stance on climate change—stronger than age, race, education, science knowledge, or even having a science degree.[8] This issue has become politically driven rather than knowledge driven, which can be frustrating for those of us who would like to make a data-driven decision but who feel inundated with political messages. Most of us are likely concerned with the state of the environment and want to do what we can to improve it. But how do we navigate between what the data actually say and the political or social agendas that often get thrown around with the data? In chapter 2, we discussed that there is a difference between science and values, yet often they get conflated in the process of communicating science. This often occurs in the case of environmental issues. Let's attempt to disentangle a few of these key controversial topics by presenting only what the science shows, devoid of any value judgments.

Is the Climate Warming?

The science decisively shows that our climate is warming and far faster (100–200 times faster) than can be attributed to normal climate cycles that have occurred in the past on our planet.[9] We have actual temperature data going back to 1880 from different areas of the world that show a gradual but exponential increase in global temperature.[10] Other sources, such as ice cores,[11] tree rings,[12] pollen in sea sediments,[13] coral, and even cave stalagmites[14] allow scientists to track the temperature of Earth going back millions of years. Each of these sources alone tell the same story—the earth is warming at a rate not previously observed. (To see the data, there are some amazing animations provided by NASA.[15])

By using all these sources (and others) combined, scientists can significantly decrease the margin of error and demonstrate historical temperatures with surprising accuracy. These data show fluctuations throughout the past, but a definitive and dramatic increase in temperature since the dawn of the industrial revolution at rates far higher than seen since the origin of our species.[16] There is a clear scientific consensus that the earth is warming at unprecedented rates. (To be clear, what causes alarm is *how quickly* global temperatures are rising rather than *where* global temperatures currently stand.)

What Are the Direct Consequences of Warming Temperatures?

There is scientific consensus that if global warming continues, we will see increases in the severity of drought and storms;[17] higher extinction rates of plant, animal, and human cultures (islands are greatly at risk);[18] and more disease and humanitarian crises.[19] Some of these consequences appear to be happening already. For humans, one of the larger threats of increasing global temperatures is the expansion of the range for infectious diseases such as malaria, cholera, dengue fever, salmonella, zika, and other diseases that are normally restricted to tropical regions.[20] Other examples include threats to marine health and sustainability,[21] melting ice sheets in the Arctic that are severely threatening polar bear populations,[22] and declining shark populations.[23]

Are Humans a Main Contributor to This Warming?

To answer this question, it is necessary to briefly explain how our planet maintains a temperature higher than outer space (which is really cold!). The earth maintains these higher temperatures through the atmosphere, which contains molecules that scientists refer to as "greenhouse gases" (these include noncondensable gases such as carbon dioxide, methane, nitrous oxide, and fluorinated gases, as well as condensable water vapor that constantly fluctuates between liquid and gaseous states).[24] As the full spectrum of sunlight enters the atmosphere, much of it is absorbed by the earth and radiated back toward space as infrared radiation (IR), which is energy with a much longer wavelength than what originally entered. This IR gets trapped by these greenhouse gases, which radiate the heat back to the earth, warming our planet.[25] The noncondensable gases directly influence the amount of water vapor in the air; thus, the more of these gases we produce, the warmer the atmosphere gets, and the more water vapor gets trapped—it is a positive feedback loop.[26]

Of the noncondensable gases in the atmosphere that contribute to this greenhouse effect, carbon dioxide is the most significant.[27] That is why it gets so much press and scientists focus on it so heavily.[28] Carbon dioxide is naturally occurring (for example, through exhaling and diffusion from the soil), but it is also produced by human activities (for example, the burning of plant materials, like fossil fuels). Scientists have closely monitored the amount of carbon dioxide in the atmosphere at locations around the globe for the past forty years.[29] They can also estimate the amount of carbon dioxide that *was* in the atmosphere up to at least 800,000 years ago.[30] The data clearly show that carbon dioxide levels have dramatically increased since the start of the industrial revolution.[31] And, as described earlier, rising carbon dioxide levels means rising global temperatures and all the determinants that come with that.

How do scientists determine where the carbon dioxide (CO_2) in the air is coming from? They use naturally occurring atoms called isotopes. Isotopes differ in the number of neutrons in their nucleus. For example, the most abundant form of carbon is carbon-12, which has six neutrons. Carbon-13 has seven neutrons, and carbon-14 has eight neutrons. Most plants have less carbon-13 than occurs in the atmosphere.[32] So scientists can simply look at the percentage of carbon-13 in the atmospheric CO_2 and can tell whether the increasing CO_2 is coming from naturally occurring sources (like exhaling and diffusion) or from the burning of plant materials.[33] Additionally, fossil plant materials (fossil fuels) completely lack the carbon-14 isotope because it decays over time; thus, the burning of fossil fuels produces a very unique isotopic signature.[34] There is a clear scientific consensus that the vast majority of extra accumulated carbon dioxide in the atmosphere is coming directly from the burning of fossil fuels.[35]

Are Animal and Plant Extinction Rates a Concern?

Mass extinction events are defined as the loss of over 75% of Earth's species at a given time.[36] Science provides strong evidence of five mass extinction events in the last 540 million years.[37] The causes of these past events were catastrophic natural events: shifts in continents, volcanic activity, global climate shifts, and meteorite impacts. Scientists have been gathering data on extinction rates today. Using a variety of techniques, scientists have found compelling evidence that extinction rates today are far above normal.[38] Since the 1500s,

85 mammal, 159 bird, 35 amphibian, and 80 fish species have gone extinct, and over 40,000 species are currently threatened with extinction (likely an underestimate).[39] There is scientific consensus that extinction rates are higher, perhaps as much as 10,000 times higher, than what would be expected from normal events, and unlike previous extinctions, there is not a catastrophic natural event to blame.

All species have inherent value as each species is God's handiwork. There are other reasons to be concerned about extinction. First, many species provide valuable and free services to humans. For example, all of our food comes directly or indirectly from plants. Those plants require pollination by insects, many of which are threatened with extinction;[40] in some areas of the world, people now have to pollinate their food crops by hand.[41] Wetland ecosystems along the coasts protect our communities from floodwater and storm surges. The extreme loss of wetlands on the coast of Louisiana directly led to the devastating effects of Hurricane Katrina.[42] Many plants and animals even provide valuable medicines such as the Gila monster, whose venom is used to treat type-2 diabetes,[43] or the horseshoe crab, whose blood is used to detect bacterial contaminations in any medicine administered by injection.[44] Additionally, marine cyanobacteria are responsible for producing 20% of the oxygen we breathe, and their existence is dependent on how healthy the oceans are.[45]

Second, many species carry important secrets of life that we may never learn if they go extinct. For example, there are 700 species of cone snails in the world that are found only on tropical coral reefs, the majority of which are in danger or have already collapsed. Together, they are thought to manufacture up to 14,000 distinct toxins that can be used for biomedical purposes; we have currently characterized only a small fraction of them.[46]

Lastly, extinction rates provide insight into how healthy our environment is. Much like the canary that coal miners brought into the mines to detect carbon monoxide (a deadly gas), the number of species extinctions we see today is our canary for the earth's health and gives us the chance to make adjustments before it is too late.

Do I Really Need to Change My Behavior?

Now that the data have been presented, let's talk about values. Thankfully, as Latter-day Saints, we have a common set of values from which we can draw. In the Doctrine and Covenants, we read, "For the earth is full, and there is enough and to spare; yea, I prepared all things, and have given unto the children of men to be agents unto themselves" (104:17). Does this guidance from the Lord mean that we can do what we please with the earth's resources? Does it mean that no matter how much we use, there will always be enough for us? Does it mean that the data about climate change or extinction rates are false or misleading? Elder Marcus B. Nash taught, "In short, the state of the human soul and the environment are interconnected, each affects and influences the other."[47] When the earth suffers, we suffer; when the earth thrives, we thrive. This truth is one reason to ponder this question about changing our behavior and to deeply examine its assumptions.

God intended that all creatures should be happy.[48] As Earth's stewards we are tasked to ensure their happiness by showing "compassion upon the earth" (Moses 7:49). What does it mean to have compassion upon the earth? Let's start with an anecdote told by a famous ecologist, Dr. Garrett Hardin.[49] The idea goes something like this: Imagine an open rangeland of specific dimensions—a "commons" area. It is shared by many cattlemen, each with an equal number of cattle on the land. Imagine a cattleman who thinks to himself, "Why not add one more cow to my herd?" This is indeed a logical thought given that the benefit to him is +1 (one more meat cow to sell at auction), and the consequence (the -1) is shared by the commons. Meaning, he doesn't experience the full weight of the consequences because he shares the effects of one extra animal on the land with *all* the cattlemen. We could think of this as similar to driving somewhere that is walkable: the benefit to us is +1, while the extra pollution in the environment goes up into the air to be shared by everyone—we probably won't even notice it. Or how about the cost of running the furnace in our homes a couple degrees warmer when cold or the air conditioner a couple degrees cooler when hot? Or the effect of one extra low-efficiency lightbulb? In each case, the benefit to us is exclusive while the detriment is shared. The tragedy comes when *everyone* uses the same logic, and *everyone* uses "one extra." Then the consequences are tragic—the tragedy of the commons.

However, and *more* importantly, the reverse is also necessarily true—when we choose *not* to indulge in "one extra," the *benefit* of our choice is shared by everyone as well. That's pretty amazing, right? Elder L. Tom Perry taught, "[The Lord] has a marvelous system of replenishment and renewal so long as we care for, conserve, and waste not."[50] We have the ability to turn things around, to work for the good of the earth, to show mercy and compassion to the plants and animals that God has created. God created this earth for us and provided ways in which it can be self-sustaining and renewable. For this to work, we simply need to be conscientious of our role by making both small and large choices to promote the health of the earth.

One Small Change

From a science *and* gospel-informed perspective we provide recommendations to foster a spirit of stewardship. These changes may not save the planet outright but the goal is to foster a spirit of stewardship in ourselves and open ourselves to scientific findings that *can* result in saving the planet. First, and foremost, it is important to recognize that even the smallest efforts can make a difference (although it almost certainly will take global cooperation to really solve it). Do what you feel like you can do now, in your current capacity. Similar to the popular story of the boy gathering starfish on the beach,[51] Jamie had a similar experience on a beach in Delaware where hundreds of horseshoe crabs become stranded with the receding tide; when this happens, they slowly suffocate and then fall prey to the sea birds standing by. Upon finding one still alive, her son picked it up, and with great effort (they are surprisingly heavy little animals), tossed it back into the waves. Did his actions make a difference? It certainly made a difference to the one he threw back. Every small act of kindness toward the earth matters, fosters a spirit of stewardship, and the Lord is certainly pleased by our efforts to honor His creations.

Reduce, Reuse, Recycle

There are so many small and simple things we can do to reduce our impact on the environment. It can be simple, like not bagging individual produce at the store. Even better would be not bagging any groceries if you can help it or making your own grocery bags from grandma's fabric stash. Cutting junk mail and recycling it when it does arrive makes a difference. Hand-me-downs are a Latter-day Saint staple within families, but making sure good clothing makes it to thrift stores or to those close to us who could use it also makes a big difference for the environment and the pocketbook. Getting, using, and keeping tabs on a single, permanent water bottle will also make an impact. Where appropriate, choosing disposable items that will biodegrade after they are discarded, like a toothbrush with a bamboo handle, can make a difference. We are sure you can think of other ways to reduce our negative impact on the environment. The most important thing is to cultivate a stewardship mindset and just try.

Energy Conservation

There are so many different options today to help with energy consumption. Some smaller actions include investing in high-efficiency lighting; turning off all lights, appliances, and technology when not in use (our teenagers struggle with this one!); walking to church or work if it's possible; encouraging our kids to walk or ride a bike to and from school; raising the temperature in our houses just one degree during the warmer months; or planning ahead to use public transportation. For some, using an alternative-fuel vehicle is an option. There are larger options when it comes to the home for those who have the resources to implement them, including installing high-efficiency appliances, windows, insulation, solar panels, and so on. Some of these larger options will save you tens of thousands of dollars over the time you own a home.

Sustainable Farming

Technology is not just limited to improving energy consumption. Technology and innovation can enhance crop yields, solve major nutrition problems, and limit the need for pesticides. This can translate to less land usage, more food, and fewer harmful chemicals in the environment. Alternative farming practices (such as permaculture and regenerative farming) can also increase native plant and animal diversity in the environment and harness free services from nature (including pollination and water retention) to decrease the cost of farming, making it even more sustainable, meaning the land can be used longer and farming impacts on the environment are smaller or even beneficial.

Growing our own gardens is also a wonderfully sustainable way to use a yard if we have one. With a garden, we require fewer of the earth's resources to feed us and water can be used more effectively on our small gardens than on larger farms. We become more independent, and we can store the food produced from our gardens, which will result in less driving. When a garden is not possible, eating few or no animal products, even for just one or two days or meals a week, will also make a difference.

Water

There is perhaps no larger concern in the world right now than water usage. It is becoming an increasingly precious resource and tightly linked to land usage. Simple actions we can take to conserve water include turning off the water while brushing teeth, shaving, soaping up in the shower, doing the dishes, and so on. Lowering the toilet bowl water level is also helpful. Larger efforts may include watering yards less and using directed water in gardens. These practices are especially vital in dry climates around the world but are still important in areas where water is pumped in. These efforts will also decrease energy consumption.

Conclusion

The earth is a gift. It is our privilege to live in such a beautiful place. The Lord spent untold time preparing a place for us to come and dwell, to learn and progress, and to experience mortality. It is no accident when something God created takes your breath away with its beauty or majesty: "All things denote there is a God; yea, even the earth and all things that are upon the face of it" (Alma 30:44). The Lord told Moses, "All things are created and made to bear record of me, both things which are temporal, and things which are spiritual; things which are in the heavens above, and things which are on the earth . . . all things bear record of me" (Moses 6:63). Striving to view "Creation Care" as a sacred responsibility while developing a spirit of stewardship within ourselves and families will bless our lives. We join with Elder Nash in saying, "This creation, every aspect of it, was created for the purpose of giving each of us the opportunity to be blessed now and in eternity. This creation witnesses of the Creator, and if we preserve these special places in their unspoiled state, they will silently, eloquently witness of our God and inspire us onward and upward."[52]

CONCLUSION

Staring out the windows of the Life Sciences Building at Brigham Young University, you can catch a glimpse of the magnificent Wasatch Mountain Range. On an October day, these mountains are arrayed in spectacular hues of orange and red as the leaves change colors, heralding the change of seasons. If anyone has had the opportunity to glimpse this sight, they might feel a desire to "stand still, and consider the wondrous works of God" (Job 37:14).

As biologists at BYU, after appreciating the beauty, we often find ourselves considering *how* God orchestrated such a beautiful scene. As we study science, we learn about the diversity of trees in the world, how they originated and how each is adapted to their individual environments. We also learn intricate details that help us explain this autumn scene and how trees begin to prepare themselves for winter as the amount of direct sunlight begins to fade in the fall. The green chlorophyll pigments break down revealing secondary red and orange pigments underneath, which capture the fringes of the visual light spectrum. To sustain themselves through the long winter months, the trees absorb any remaining nutrients from the leaves and build a protective seal between the leaves and their branches, causing the leaves to eventually die and drop from the trees.[1] Though perhaps less poetic, this view of tre
and the explanation for fall colors still moves us. The d
of trees and the processes they undergo to adap
ronments is eloquent, effectual, and divine.

Viewing this scene from a religious perspecti

us that God is the Creator, and that "all things which [God] had made were very good" (Moses 2:31). It also teaches us that God loves us enough to spend an enormous amount of time and care to create this earth as a gift for His children. David declared, "When I consider thy heavens, the work of thy fingers, the moon and the stars, which thou hast ordained; What is man, that thou art mindful of him?" (Psalm 8:3–4).

Viewing this scene from a scientific perspective leaves us in awe of God's great power and the wisdom of His workmanship. Scientific knowledge does not lessen but strengthens our testimony of the divinity of our Creator. The Lord taught, "All things are created and made to bear record of me, both things which are temporal, and things which are spiritual; things which are in the heavens above, and things which are on the earth, and things which are in the earth, and things which are under the earth, both above and beneath: all things bear record of me" (Moses 6:63).

Using the thinking patterns laid out in part 1 can help us embrace the knowledge we gain from science in a way that is in harmony with, rather than in contradiction to, our spiritual understanding. First, understanding how science is done and acknowledging both its capacity and limitations can help us more fully integrate scientific knowledge with our faith. Second, learning to differentiate between scientific data and value-based interpretations, as well as keeping an agnostic perspective of science, can facilitate productive dialogue as we learn. Third, basing our faith in God on spiritual evidence rather than setting up a "God of the Gaps" can protect our testimonies from potential refutation by scientific discovery. Fourth, by teaching correct science in our homes, bathed in the light of the gospel, we can protect ourselves from pseudoscientific viewpoints that may shake testimonies. And fifth, by increasing our comfort with uncertainty, we can avoid the doubt that we might be tempted to feel when things we learn seem to conflict with our beliefs. Lastly, by fully considering the science laid out in part 2 and discussing it openly with our families, we help prepare ourselves and our loved ones to combat the secular ideas that mistakenly pit science against our religious faith. With patience and diligence, we can enrich our understanding of the natural world while increasing our testimony of God.

As we seek to reconcile science and religion, we can more fully see the hand of God in our lives. It is our testimony that a clear understanding of the way in which science and religion work together can bring us closer to truth and closer to God. And we can declare together, as we look upon the wonder and majesty of the natural world, with both spiritual and scientific eyes, that we have "seen God moving in his majesty and power" (Doctrine and Covenants 88:47).

FURTHER READING

The Nature of Science

Oreskes, Naomi. *Why Trust Science?* Princeton, NJ: Princeton University Press, 2019.

Peck, Steven L. *Science the Key to Theology, Volume One: Preliminaries*. Salt Lake City: BCC Press, 2017.

Wilson, Edward O. *Consilience: The Unity of Knowledge*. New York: Vintage Books, 1999.

Ways to Reconcile Science and Religion

Collins, Francis. *Language of God*. New York: Free Press, 2006.

Haught, John. *Science and Faith: A New Introduction*. New York: Paulist Press, 2012.

McGrath, Alister E. *Inventing the Universe: Why We Can't Stop Talking about Science, Faith, and God*. London: Hodder and Stoughton, 2015.

Polkinghorne, John C. *The Faith of a Physicist*. Princeton, NJ: Princeton University Press, 1994.

Sacks, Jonathan. *The Great Partnership: Science, Religion, and the Search for Meaning*. New York: Schocken Books, 2012.

Evolution

Giberson, Karl. *Seven Glorious Days: A Scientist Retells the Genesis Creation Story*. Orleans, MA: Paraclete Press, 2012.

Grabbe, Lester L. *Faith and Fossils: The Bible, Creation, and Evolution*. Grand Rapids, MI: Wm. B. Eerdmans Publishing Co., 2018.

Greenwood, Kyle R., ed. *Since the Beginning: Interpreting Genesis 1 and 2 through the Ages*. Ada, MI: Baker Academic, 2018.

Harari, Yuval Noah. *Sapiens: A Brief History of Humankind*. New York: Vintage Books, 2011.

National Academy of Sciences. *Science and Creationism: A View from the National Academy of Sciences*. 2nd ed. Washington, DC: The National Academies Press, 1999.

Shubin, Neil. *Your Inner Fish: A Journey into the 3.5-Billion-Year History of the Human Body*. New York: Vintage Books, 2008.

Swamidass, S. Joshua. *The Genealogical Adam and Eve*. Dowers Grove, IL: InterVarsity Press, 2019.

Health and Medical Science

Hotez, Peter J. *Vaccines Did Not Cause Rachel's Autism: My Journey as a Vaccine Scientist, Pediatrician, and Autism Dad*. Baltimore: Johns Hopkins University Press, 2018.

Walker, Matthew. *Why We Sleep*. New York: Scribner, 2017.

Nature versus Nurture

Plomin, Robert. *Blueprint: How DNA Makes Us Who We Are*. Cambridge, MA: MIT Press, 2018.

Environmental Stewardship

Brown, William P. *The Seven Pillars of Creation: The Bible, Science, and the Ecology of Wonder*. New York: Oxford University Press, 2010.

Goodall, Jane, and Phillip Berman. *Reason for Hope: A Spiritual Journey*. New York: Grand Central Publishing, 1999.

Handley, George B. *The Hope of Nature: Our Care for God's Creations*. Provo, UT: Neal A. Maxwell Institute, 2020.

Hayhoe, Katharine. *Saving Us: A Climate Scientist's Case for Hope and Healing in a Divided World*. New York: Atria/One Signal Publishers, 2021.

Maathai, Wangari. *Replenishing the Earth: Spiritual Values for Healing Ourselves and the World*. New York: Doubleday Religion, 2010.

NOTES

Epigraph

Russell M. Nelson, as quoted in Marianne Holman Prescott, "Church Leaders Gather at BYU's Life Sciences Building for Dedication," *Church News,* April 17, 2015, ChurchofJesusChrist.org.

Introduction

1. "Religion among the Millennials," Pew Research, February 17, 2010, https://www.pewresearch.org/religion/2010/02/17/religion-among-the-millennials/.
2. "10 Key Findings about the Religious Lives of U.S. Teens and Their Parents," Pew Research, September 10, 2020, https://www.pewresearch.org/fact-tank/2020/09/10/10-key-findings-about-the-religious-lives-of-u-s-teens-and-their-parents/.
3. Joseph Smith to Isaac Galland, March 22, 1839, Liberty Jail, Liberty, Missouri, published in *Times and Seasons,* February 1840, 53–54; spelling and grammar modernized.

Chapter 1: The Nature and Limitations of Science as a Way of Knowing

1. For a more detailed discussion of the nature of science, see Naomi Oreskies, *Why Trust Science?* (Princeton, NJ: Princeton University Press, 2019); Steven L. Peck, *Science the Key to Theology, Volume One: Preliminaries* (Salt Lake City: BCC Press, 2017); Edward O. Wilson, *Consilience: The Unity of Knowledge* (New York: Vintage Books, 1999).
2. National Academy of Sciences, *Science and Creationism: A View from the National Academy of Sciences*, 2nd ed. (Washington, DC: The National Academies Press, 1999), https://doi.org/10.17226/6024. See also "Understanding Science 101," Understanding Science, University of California, Berkeley, accessed September 1, 2022, https://undsci.berkeley.edu/article/0_0_0/howscienceworks_19.
3. *Cambridge Dictionary*, s.v. "Assumption," accessed September 1, 2022, https://dictionary.cambridge.org/us/dictionary/english/assumption.
4. For a more in-depth description along with instructional materials, visit "Basic Assumptions of Science," on UC Berkeley's website Understanding Science, https://undsci.berkeley.edu/article/basic_assumptions.

5. *Encyclopaedia Britannica*, s.v. "Phlogiston," last modified April 24, 2017, https://www.britannica.com/science/phlogiston.
6. "The Chemical Revolution of Antoine-Laurent Lavoisier," American Chemical Society, accessed September 2, 2022, https://www.acs.org/education/whatischemistry/landmarks/lavoisier.html.
7. D. Todd Christofferson, "Truth Endures" (address to CES religious educators, January 26, 2018), https://www.churchofjesuschrist.org/broadcasts/article/evening-with-a-general-authority/2018/01/truth-endures.
8. Please note that we did not name this framework, and we realize it is an unfortunate (although poignant) acronym; Sarah Blakeslee, "The CRAAP Test," *LOEX Quarterly* 31, no. 3 (2004), https://commons.emich.edu/loexquarterly/vol31/iss3/4.

Chapter 2: Science Is Agnostic

1. For example, see M. Elizabeth Barnes et al., "'Accepting Evolution Means You Can't Believe in God': Atheistic Perceptions of Evolution among College Biology Students," *CBE—Life Sciences Education* 19, no. 2 (2020), https://doi.org/10.1187/cbe.19-05-0106.
2. Daniel C. Fisher et al., "Anatomy, Death, and Preservation of a Woolly Mammoth (*Mammuthus primigenius*) Calf, Yamal Peninsula, Northwest Siberia," *Quaternary International* 255 (March 2012): 94–105, https://doi.org/10.1016/j.quaint.2011.05.040.
3. "The Life of Dolly," The Roslin Institute, accessed September 2, 2022, https://dolly.roslin.ed.ac.uk/facts/the-life-of-dolly/index.html.
4. Nadin Rohland et al., "Proboscidean Mitogenomics: Chronology and Mode of Elephant Evolution Using Mastodon as Outgroup," *PLoS Biology* 5, no. 207, (2007), https://doi.org/10.1371/journal.pbio.0050207.
5. Patrick D. Hsu, Eric S. Lander, and Feng Zhang, "Development and Applications of CRISPR-Cas9 for Genome Engineering," *Cell* 157, no. 6, (2014): 1262–78, https://doi.org/10.1016/j.cell.2014.05.010.
6. Laura DeFrancesco, "Church to De-Extinct Woolly Mammoths," *Nature Biotechnology* 39, no. 1171 (2021): 1169–75, https://doi.org/10.1038/s41587-021-01096-y.
7. "Species Directory," World Wildlife Fund, accessed September 2, 2022, https://www.worldwildlife.org/species/directory?direction=desc&sort=extinction_status.
8. For examples, see Riley Black, "Woolly Mammoths Roamed Far and Wide Just Like Living Elephants," Smithsonian Institution, August 12, 2021, https://www.smithsonianmag.com/science-nature/woolly-mammoths-roamed-far-and-wide-just-living-elephants-180978418/; James A. Fellows Yates et al., "Central European Woolly Mammoth Population Dynamics: Insights from Late Pleistocene Mitochondrial Genomes," *Scientific Reports* 7, no. 17714 (2017), https://doi.org/10.1038/s41598-017-17723-1.
9. See K. H. Campbell et al., "Cloning: Eight Years after Dolly," *Reproduction in Domestic Animals* 40, no. 4 (July 2005): 256–68, https://doi.org/10.1111/j.1439-0531.2005.00591.x; J. Folch et al., "First Birth

of an Animal from an Extinct Subspecies (*Capra pyrenaica pyrenaica*) by Cloning," *Theriogenology* 71, no. 6 (April 2009): 1026–34, https://doi.org/10.1016/j.theriogenology.2008.11.005.

10. Dan M. Kahan et al., "Culture and Identity-Protective Cognition: Explaining the White-Male Effect in Risk Perception," *Journal of Empirical Legal Studies* 4, no. 3 (2007): 465–505, https://doi.org/10.1111/j.1740-1461.2007.00097.x.
11. For a wonderful video explaining how scientists know that the increasing carbon dioxide is human caused, see "The Science of Climate Change" (video), BioInteractive, https://www.biointeractive.org/classroom-resources/science-climate-change.
12. "Values," Ethics Unwrapped, The University of Texas at Austin, accessed September 6, 2022, https://ethicsunwrapped.utexas.edu/glossary/values.
13. See "The Family: A Proclamation to the World," ChurchofJesusChrist.org.
14. Eugenie Scott, *Evolution vs. Creationism: An Introduction*, 2nd ed. Berkley: (Oakland: University of California Press, 2009), 63–64.
15. The age of the earth is calculated through several triangulating methods, all relying on radiometric dating techniques, or analysis of radioactive isotopes in rocks. These dates have been obtained from the oldest rocks and zircon crystals found on our planet, as well as from dating moon rocks and meteorites. Scientists are confident in a 4.54 billion-year-old earth with 1% uncertainty. For more information, see "Age of the Earth," USGS, https://pubs.usgs.gov/gip/geotime/age.html; Colin Schultz, "How Do We Know the Earth Is 4.6 Billion Years Old?," *Smithsonian*, May 16, 2014, https://www.smithsonianmag.com/smart-news/how-do-we-know-earth-46-billion-years-old-180951483/; "How Old Is the Earth?," BioLogos, May 16, 2015, https://biologos.org/resources/how-old-is-the-earth.
16. Similar to dating the earth, scientists look for the oldest evidence of lifeforms. The oldest evidence they have found are layers of sediment that form through bacterial activity called stromatolites along with carbon isotopes that are indicative of living things. The oldest stromatolites found are 3.5 billion years old. For more information, see "Early Life on Earth—Animal Origins," National Museum of Natural History, https://naturalhistory.si.edu/education/teaching-resources/life-science/early-life-earth-animal-origins#:~:text=The%20earliest%20life%20forms%20we,is%20produced%20by%20living%20things. See also Andrew H. Knoll et al., "Life: The First Two Billion Years," *Philosophical Transactions of the Royal Society of London. Series B, Biological Sciences* 371, no. 1707 (2016): 20150493, https://doi.org/10.1098/rstb.2015.0493.
17. Barnes et al., "Accepting Evolution Means You Can't Believe in God."
18. Spencer W. Kimball, "Seek Learning, Even by Study and Also by Faith," *Ensign*, September 1983, ChurchofJesusChrist.org.
19. Kimball, "Seek Learning."

20. Dallin H. Oaks, "Truth and the Plan," *Ensign* or *Liahona*, November 2018, 25, ChurchofJesusChrist.org.

Chapter 3: Base Your Faith in God on Correct Evidence

1. See "Chastity" and "Environmental Stewardship and Conservation," Gospel Topics, topics.ChurchofJesusChrist.org.
2. Colette Hemingway and Seán Hemingway, "Greek Gods and Religious Practices," *Heilbrunn Timeline of Art History*, The Metropolitan Museum of Art, October 2003, https://www.metmuseum.org/toah/hd/grlg/hd_grlg.htm.
3. "Lightning," National Geographic, accessed September 6, 2022, https://www.nationalgeographic.com/environment/article/lightning#:~:text=Lightning%20is%20an%20electrical%20discharge,%2C%20ribbon%2C%20or%20rocket%20lightning.
4. "What Is an Earthquake and What Causes Them to Happen?," United States Geological Survey, accessed October 25, 2022, https://www.usgs.gov/faqs/what-earthquake-and-what-causes-them-happen.
5. Robert Mendelsohn, "What Causes Crop Failure?," *Climatic Change* 81 (2007): 61–70, https://doi.org/10.1007/s10584-005-9009-y.
6. D. C. Lindberg, *The Beginnings of Western Science* (Chicago: University of Chicago Press, 1992).
7. See J. G. M. Thewissen et al., "From Land to Water: The Origin of Whales, Dolphins, and Porpoises," *Evolution: Education and Outreach* 2, no. 2 (2009): 272–88, https://doi.org/10.1007/s12052-009-0135-2.
8. J. G. M. Thewissen et al., "Developmental Basis for Hind-Limb Loss in Dolphins and Origin of the Cetacean Bodyplan," *Proceedings of the National Academy of Sciences USA* 103, no. 22 (2006): 8414–18, https://doi.org/10.1073/pnas.0602920103.
9. C. G. J. Petersen, "The Motion of Whales during Swimming," *Nature* 116 (1925): 327–29.
10. J. G. M. Thewissen et al., "Eocene Mammal Faunas from Northern Indo-Pakistan," *Journal of Vertebrate Paleontology* 21, no. 2 (2001): 347–66, https://doi.org/10.1671/0272-4634(2001)021[0347:EMFFNI]2.0.CO;2.
11. Thewissen et al., "Developmental Basis for Hind Limb Loss," 8414–18.
12. Philip D. Gingerich et al., "New Whale from the Eocene of Pakistan and the Origin of Cetacean Swimming," *Nature* 368, (1994): 844–47, https://doi.org/10.1038/368844a0.
13. Mark D. Uhen, "Middle to Late Eocene Basilosaurines and Dorudontines," in *The Emergence of Whales: Evolutionary Patterns in the Origin of Cetacea*, ed. J. G. M. Thewissen (New York: Plenum, 1998), 29–61.
14. E. A. Buchholtz, "Implications of Vertebral Morphology for Locomotor Evolution in Early Cetacea," in *The Emergence of Whales*, 325–51.
15. Thewissen et al., "From Land to Water," 272–88.
16. Masato Nikaido et al., "Phylogenetic Relationships among Cetartiodactyls Based on Insertions of Short and Long Interspersed Elements: Hippopotamuses Are the Closest Extant Relatives of Whales,"

Proceedings of the National Academy of Sciences 96, no. 18 (1999): 10261–66, https://doi.org/10.1073/pnas.96.18.10261.

17. "Sperm Whales' Amazing Adaptations," American Museum of Natural History, April 15, 2013, https://www.amnh.org/explore/news-blogs/on-exhibit-posts/sperm-whales-amazing-adaptations.
18. For example, see John Struthers, "On the Rudimentary Hind-Limb of a Great Fin-Whale (*Balaenoptera Musculus*) in Comparison with Those of the Humpback Whale and the Greenland Right-Whale," *Journal of Anatomy and Physiology* 27, no. 3 (1893): 291–335, https://pubmed.ncbi.nlm.nih.gov/17232044/.
19. US Declaration of Independence, 1776.
20. Kristen Renwick Monroe, "Biology, Psychology, Ethics, and Politics: An Innate Moral Sense?," chap. 45 in *On Human Nature*, ed. Michael Tibayrenc and Francisco J. Ayala (Cambridge, MA: Academic Press, 2017), 757–70.
21. B. Kenward and M. Dahl, "Preschoolers Distribute Scarce Resources According to the Moral Valence of Recipients' Previous Actions," *Developmental Psychology* 47, no. 4 (2011): 1054–64, https://doi.org/10.1037/a0023869; Rimma Teper, Michael Inzlicht, and Elizabeth Page-Gould, "Are We More Moral Than We Think? Exploring the Role of Affect in Moral Behavior and Moral Forecasting," *Psychological Science* 22, no. 4 (2011): 553–58, https://doi.org/10.1177/0956797611402513.
22. See Douglas Allchin, "The Evolution of Morality," *Evolution: Education and Outreach* 2 (2009): 590–601, https://doi.org/10.1007/s12052-009-0167-7.
23. See, for examples, T. H. Clutton-Brock et al., "Selfish Sentinels in Cooperative Mammals," *Science* 284, no. 5420 (1999): 1640–44, https://doi.org/10.1126/science.284.5420.1640; W. D. Hamilton, "The Genetical Evolution of Social Behavior," *Journal of Theoretical Biology* 7, no. 1 (1964): 17–52; Frans de Waal, *Good Natured: The Origins of Right and Wrong in Humans and Other Animals* (Cambridge: Harvard University Press, 1996); Dale J. Langford et al., "Social Modulation of Pain as Evidence of Empathy in Mice," *Science* 312, no. 5782 (2006): 1967–70, https://www.science.org/doi/10.1126/science.1128322.
24. Dallin H. Oaks, "Testimony," *Ensign* or *Liahona*, May 2008, 26, ChurchofJesusChrist.org.
25. Oaks, "Testimony," 26.
26. Oaks, "Testimony," 26.

Chapter 4: Teach True Science, Not Pseudoscience

1. For an extensive review, see Brian Deer, "How the Case against the MMR Vaccine Was Fixed," *BMJ* 342, no. 1 (2011): c5347, https://doi.org/10.1136/bmj.c5347.
2. Julia Belluz, "Research Fraud Catalyzed the Anti-Vaccination Movement. Let's Not Repeat History," *Vox*, March 5, 2019, https://www.vox.com/2018/2/27/17057990/andrew-wakefield-vaccines-autism-study; Matthew Motta and Dominik Stecula, "Quantifying the Effect of Wakefield et al. (1998) on Skepticism about MMR

Vaccine Safety in the U.S.," *PLoS One* 16, no.8 (2021), https://doi.org/10.1371/journal.pone.0256395.

3. "Global, Regional, and National Age–Sex Specific All-Cause and Cause-Specific Mortality for 240 Causes of Death, 1990–2013: A Systematic Analysis for the Global Burden of Disease Study 2013," *Lancet* 385 (2015): 117–71, www.thelancet.com/pdfs/journals/lancet/PIIS0140-6736(14)61682-2.pdf.
4. For the full story, see Loren Graham, *Lysenko's Ghost* (Cambridge: Harvard University Press, 2016).
5. Personal communication, used with permission.
6. Pew Research Center, "Religion among the Millennials," accessed September 14, 2022, https://www.pewresearch.org/religion/2010/02/17/religion-among-the-millennials/.
7. Scott Esplin (address, BYU Aspen Grove Family Camp, July 2021).
8. See the Gospel Topics Essays at https://www.churchofjesuschrist.org/study/manual/gospel-topics-essays?lang=eng.
9. "Gospel Topics Essays," https://www.churchofjesuschrist.org/study/manual/gospel-topics-essays/essays?lang=eng.
10. M. Elizabeth Barnes and Sara E. Brownell, "A Call to Use Cultural Competence When Teaching Evolution to Religious College Students," *CBE—Life Sciences Education* 16, no. 4 (2018), https://doi.org/10.1187/cbe.17-04-0062.
11. John Lindsay et al., "Using a Reconciliation Module Leads to Large Gains in Evolution Acceptance," *CBE—Life Sciences Education* 18, no. 4 (2019), https://doi.org/10.1187/cbe.19-04-0080; Daniel G. Ferguson and Jamie L. Jensen, "Role Models, Compatibility, and Knowledge Lead to Increased Evolution Acceptance," *Evolution: Education and Outreach* 14, no. 16 (2021), https://doi.org/10.1186/s12052-021-00155-x.
12. Ethan R. Tolman et al., "Reconciling Evolution: Evidence from a Biology and Theology Course," *Evolution: Education and Outreach* 13, no. 19 (2020), https://doi.org/10.1186/s12052-020-00133-9.
13. Ethan R. Tolman et al., "Testing the Effect of Aquarium-Based Learning on Patron Acceptance of Evolutionary Theory," *Journal of Zoo and Aquarium Research* 9, no. 2 (2021): 102–9. https://doi.org/10.19227/jzar.v9i2.542.
14. Mahealani Kaloi et al., "Exploring the Relationship between Science, Religion, and Attitudes toward Evolution Education," *American Biology Teacher* 84, no. 2 (2022): 75–81, https://doi.org/10.1525/abt.2022.84.2.75.
15. See statements by Russell M. Nelson in "Life Sciences Building Dedicated," Brigham Young University, accessed March 15, 2023, https://lifesciences.byu.edu/life-sciences-building-dedicated.
16. *Teachings of Presidents of the Church: Brigham Young* (1997), 15.

Chapter 5: Comfort with Uncertainty

1. Colin Camerer and Martin Weber, "Recent Developments in Modeling Preferences: Uncertainty and Ambiguity," *Journal of Risk*

and Uncertainty 5, no. 4 (1992): 325–70, https://www.jstor.org/stable/41755006.

2. Laurie R. Santos and Alexandra G. Rosati, "The Evolutionary Roots of Human Decision Making," *Annual Review of Psychology* 66 (2015): 321-47, https://doi.org/10.1146/annurev-psych-010814-015310.
3. "Autoimmune Disorders," MedlinePlus, accessed September 13, 2022, https://medlineplus.gov/ency/article/000816.htm.
4. "Understanding How Vaccines Work," Centers for Disease Control and Prevention, last modified May 23, 2022, https://www.cdc.gov/vaccines/hcp/conversations/understanding-vacc-work.html.
5. "Species," National Museum of Natural History, accessed September 13, 2022, https://humanorigins.si.edu/evidence/human-fossils/species.
6. J. B. van Helmont, *Oriatrike or Physick Refined*, trans. John Chandler (London: Lodowick Loyd, 1662).
7. See "Discovery of Photosynthesis," Photosynthesis Education, https://photosynthesiseducation.com/discovery-of-photosynthesis/.
8. An isotope is an atom with different numbers of protons; in this case, they used oxygen atoms that contained twelve neutrons instead of the typical six neutrons.
9. Samuel Ruben et al., "Heavy Oxygen (O^{18}) as a Tracer in the Study of Photosynthesis," *Journal of the American Chemical Society* 63, no. 3 (1941): 877–79, https://doi.org/10.1021/ja01848a512.
10. Karin Nickelsen, *Explaining Photosynthesis: Models of Biochemical Mechanisms, 1840–1960* (Dordrecht: Springer, 2015).
11. Pierre C. Hohenberg, "Science, Religion and the Teaching of Evolution," arXiv, Cornell University, August 2010, 2, https://arxiv.org/ftp/arxiv/papers/1704/1704.03023.pdf.
12. Hohenberg, "Science, Religion and the Teaching of Evolution," 2.
13. "Basics of COVID-19," Centers for Disease Control and Prevention, last modified November 4, 2021, https://www.cdc.gov/coronavirus/2019-ncov/your-health/about-covid-19/basics-covid-19.html.
14. For a simple explanation of immunity, see "Immune System," Kids Health, reviewed October 2019, https://kidshealth.org/en/parents/immune.html.
15. Geoffrey D. Munro, "The Scientific Impotence Excuse: Discounting Belief-Threatening Scientific Abstracts," *Journal of Applied Social Psychology* 40, no. 3 (2010): 579–600, https://doi.org/10.1111/j.1559-1816.2010.00588.x.
16. A. S. Hornby, ed., *Oxford Advanced Learner's Dictionary of Current English* (Oxford: Oxford University Press, 1995).
17. Dieter F. Uchtdorf, "What Is Truth?" (Continuing Education broadcast, January 13, 2013), https://www.churchofjesuschrist.org/broadcasts/article/ces-devotionals/2013/01/what-is-truth?
18. For an overview, see Harold Ellis, "Ignaz Semmelweis: Tragic Pioneer in the Prevention of Puerperal Sepsis," *British Journal of Hospital Medicine (London)* 69, no. 6 (2008): 358, https://doi.org/10.12968/hmed.2008.69.6.29631; Ian R. Daniels, "Historical Perspectives on

Health. Semmelweis: A Lesson to Relearn?" *Journal of the Royal Society for the Promotion of Health* 118, no. 6 (1998): 367–70, https://doi.org/10.1177/146642409811800617.

19. Russell M. Nelson, "Where Is Wisdom?" *Ensign,* November 1992, 7, ChurchofJesusChrist.org.
20. DoSER is the Dialogue on Science, Ethics, and Religion run by the American Association for the Advancement of Science. It encourages fruitful dialogue between scientific and religious organizations; Dr. Burnett currently works for the Templeton Foundation, a foundation that funds scientific research at its intersection with faith.
21. Thomas Burnett, "What Is Scientism?" American Association for the Advancement of Science, May 21, 2012, aaas.org/programs/dialogue-science-ethics-and-religion/what-scientism.
22. Henry M. Morris, *The Twilight of Evolution* (Grand Rapids, MI: Baker Book House, 1964), 56.
23. *The Udāna; or, The Solemn Utterances of the Buddha,* translated from the Pali by D. M. Strong (London: Luzac and Company, 1902), 93–96.
24. Uchtdorf, "What Is Truth?"

Chapter 6: Evolution

1. Joseph F. Smith, John R. Winder, and Anthon H. Lund, "The Origin of Man," *Improvement Era* 13 (November 1909): 75–61.
2. Joseph F. Smith, "Philosophy and the Church Schools," *Juvenile Instructor* 46, no. 4 (April 1911): 208–9. Heber J. Grant, Anthony W. Ivins, and Charles W. Nibley, "'Mormon' View of Evolution: 1925 First Presidency Message," https://josephsmithfoundation.org/docs/mormon-view-of-evolution-1925-first-presidency-message/.
3. First Presidency, memorandum to General Authorities, April 1931.
4. "What Does the Church Believe about Evolution?" *New Era,* October 2016, ChurchofJesusChrist.org; see also First Presidency, "'Mormon' View of Evolution," 1925.
5. "Organic Evolution," Church History Topics, accessed November 25, 2022, https://www.churchofjesuschrist.org/study/history/topics/organic-evolution?lang=eng.
6. For more information on appropriate interpretations of these texts, see Todd Patterson, "Genesis 1:1–2:3: The Creation Account as Hebrew Poiesis," January 21, 2010, https://www.toddjana.com/genesis-11-23-the-creation-account-as-hebrew-poiesis/; "How to Read the Bible," BibleProject, accessed February 13, 2023, https://bibleproject.com/explore/how-to-read-the-bible/; John H. Walton, *The Lost World of Genesis One: Ancient Cosmology and the Origins Debate* (Downers Grove, IL: InterVarsity Press, 2009).
7. "Age of the Earth," United States Geological Survey, last modified July 9, 2007, https://pubs.usgs.gov/gip/geotime/age.html.
8. Stephen Moorbath, "Dating Earliest Life," *Nature* 434, no. 155 (2005), https://doi.org/10.1038/434155a.

9. Eduardo Kac, "GFP Bunny," *Leonardo* 36, no. 2 (2003): 97–102, http://www.jstor.org/stable/1577432.
10. Guy Drouin et al., "The Genetics of Vitamin C Loss in Vertebrates," *Current Genomics* 12, no. 5, (2011): 371–78, https://doi.org/10.2174/138920211796429736.
11. Riley Black, "What Could Live in a Real Jurassic World? A Chickenosaurus," *National Geographic*, June 18, 2015, https://www.nationalgeographic.com/animals/article/150618-jurassic-world-genetic-engineering-chickenosaurus.
12. Neal Anthwal, Leena Joshi, and Abigail S. Tucker, "Evolution of the Mammalian Middle Ear and Jaw: Adaptations and Novel Structures," *Journal of Anatomy* 222, no. 1 (2013): 147–60, https://doi.org/10.1111/j.1469-7580.2012.01526.x.
13. Sayaka Tojima, "A Tale of the Tail: A Comprehensive Understanding of the 'Human Tail,'" *Journal of Korean Neurosurgical Society* 64, no. 3 (2021): 340–45, https://doi.org/10.3340/jkns.2021.0017.
14. J. G. M. Thewissen et al., "Developmental Basis for Hind-Limb Loss in Dolphins and Origin of the Cetacean Bodyplan," *Proceedings of the National Academy of Sciences* 103, no. 22 (2006): 8414–18, https://doi.org/10.1073/pnas.0602920103.
15. Florian Maderspacher, "Evolution: Flight of the Ratites," *Current Biology* 27, no. 3 (2017): R110–13, https://doi.org/10.1016/j.cub.2016.12.023.
16. Eugenie Scott, *Evolution vs. Creationism: An Introduction*, 2nd ed. (Berkeley: University of California Press, 2009), 63–64.
17. For a good review of theistic evolution, also referred to as "evolutionary creationism," see Ted Davis, "Theistic Evolution: History and Beliefs," BioLogos, October 15, 2012, https://biologos.org/series/science-and-the-bible/articles/theistic-evolution-history-and-beliefs.
18. Michael W. Nachman et al., "The Genetic Basis of Adaptive Melanism in Pocket Mice," *Proceedings of the National Academy of Sciences* 100, no. 9 (2003): 5268–73, https://doi.org/10.1073/pnas.0431157100.
19. For a fascinating review, see "The Evolution of Whales," University of California Museum of Paleontology, last modified June 2020, https://evolution.berkeley.edu/what-are-evograms/the-evolution-of-whales/.
20. Michael Yarus, "Getting Past the RNA World: The Initial Darwinian Ancestor," *Cold Spring Harbor Perspectives in Biology* 3, no. 4 (2011), https://www.ncbi.nlm.nih.gov/pmc/articles/PMC3062219/.
21. Madeline C. Weiss et al., "The Physiology and Habitat of the Last Universal Common Ancestor," *Nature Microbiology* 1 (2016), https://doi.org/10.1038/nmicrobiol.2016.116.
22. First Presidency letter, *Improvement Era* 28 (September 1925): 11.
23. "What Does the Church Believe about Evolution?" *New Era,* October 2016; see also First Presidency, "'Mormon' View of Evolution," 1925.
24. Spencer W. Kimball, "The Blessings and Responsibilities of Womanhood," *Ensign*, March 1976, 70–72, ChurchofJesusChrist.org.
25. For example, Yuval Noah Harari, *Sapiens: A Brief History of*

Humankind (New York: Vintage Books, 2011); Neil Shubin, *Your Inner Fish: A Journey into the 3.5-Billion-Year History of the Human Body* (New York: Vintage Books, 2008).

26. "Homo Sapiens," National Museum of Natural History, last modified January 22, 2021, https://humanorigins.si.edu/evidence/human-fossils/species/homo-sapiens.
27. For an overview, see Lisa Hendry, "Who Were the Neanderthals?" Natural History Museum, accessed February 14, 2023, https://www.nhm.ac.uk/discover/who-were-the-neanderthals.html.
28. "*Homo Naledi*," National Museum of Natural History, last modified July 1, 2022, https://humanorigins.si.edu/evidence/human-fossils/species/homo-naledi.
29. "Origin of Man," *Improvement Era* 13 (April 1910): 57.
30. Natalie Angier, "Do Races Differ? Not Really, Genes Show," *New York Times*, August 22, 2000, https://www.nytimes.com/2000/08/22/science/do-races-differ-not-really-genes-show.html.
31. See Stephen Richmond et al., "Facial Genetics: A Brief Overview," *Frontiers in Genetics* 9 (2018), https://doi.org/10.3389/fgene.2018.00462.
32. Theresa M. Duello et al., "Race and Genetics versus 'Race' in Genetics: A Systematic Review of the Use of African Ancestry in Genetic Studies," *Evolution, Medicine, and Public Health* 9, no. 1 (2021): 232–45, https://doi.org/10.1093/emph/eoab018.
33. "Race Relations," Newsroom, The Church of Jesus Christ of Latter-day Saints, 2008, https://newsroom.churchofjesuschrist.org/topic/race-relations.
34. Russell M. Nelson, as quoted in Marianne Holman Prescott, "Church Leaders Gather at BYU's Life Sciences Building for Dedication," *Church News*, April 17, 2015.
35. Dallin H. Oaks, *Life's Lessons Learned: Personal Reflections* (Salt Lake City: Deseret Book, 2011).

Chapter 7: Health and Medical Science

1. "FY 2022 Spending by Agency," USASpending, last modified July 31, 2022, https://www.usaspending.gov/explorer/agency.
2. "Budget," National Institutes of Health, last modified August 18, 2022, https://www.nih.gov/about-nih/what-we-do/budget#:~:text=Grants%20Awarded&text=*%20This%20amount%20reflects%20the%20sum,million%20for%20Superfund%20Research%20activities.
3. "About NIH," National Institutes of Health, accessed September 13, 2022, https://www.nih.gov/about-nih.
4. "The Family: A Proclamation to the World," ChurchofJesusChrist.org.
5. Erica D. Sonnenburg et al., "Diet-Induced Extinctions in the Gut Microbiota Compound over Generations," *Nature* 529, no. 7585 (2016): 212–15, https://doi.org/10.1038/nature16504.
6. For example, Marion Valle et al., "Differential Effects of Chronic Ingestion of Refined Sugars versus Natural Sweeteners on Insulin

Resistance and Hepatic Steatosis in a Rat Model of Diet-Induced Obesity," *Nutrients* 12, no. 8 (2020): 2292, https://doi.org/10.3390/nu12082292; and see, for an overview, "Natural vs. Refined Sugars: What's the Difference?" City of Hope, October 26, 2022, https://www.cancercenter.com/community/blog/2016/08/natural-vs-refined-sugars-what-is-the-difference.

7. Peter J. Huth et al., "Major Food Sources of Calories, Added Sugars, and Saturated Fat and Their Contribution to Essential Nutrient Intakes in the U.S. Diet," *Nutrition Journal* 12, no. 116 (2013), https://doi.org/10.1186/1475-2891-12-116.
8. For example, Luigi Castaldo et al., "Red Wine Consumption and Cardiovascular Health," *Molecules* 24, no. 19 (2019): 3626, https://doi.org/10.3390/molecules24193626.
9. GBD 2016 Alcohol Collaborators, "Alcohol Use and Burden for 195 Countries and Territories, 1990–2016," *The Lancet* 392, no. 10152 (2018): 1015–35, https://doi.org/10.1016/S0140-6736(18)31310-2.
10. *General Handbook: Serving in The Church of Jesus Christ of Latter-day Saints*, 38.7.14, ChurchofJesusChrist.org.
11. Rob M. van Dam et al., "Coffee, Caffeine, and Health," *New England Journal of Medicine* 383, no. 4 (2020): 369–78, https://doi.org/10.1056/NEJMra1816604.
12. Farhad Islami et al., "High-Temperature Beverages and Foods and Esophageal Cancer Risk," *International Journal of Cancer* 125, no. 3 (2009): 491–524, https://doi.org/10.1002/ijc.24445.
13. Matthew Walker, *Why We Sleep: Unlocking the Power of Sleep and Dreams* (New York: Scribner Books, 2017).
14. American Cancer Society, *Cancer Facts & Figures 2021* (Atlanta: American Cancer Society, 2021), https://www.cancer.org/content/dam/cancer-org/research/cancer-facts-and-statistics/annual-cancer-facts-and-figures/2021/cancer-facts-and-figures-2021.pdf.
15. For an overview, see Jed Woodworth, "The Word of Wisdom," in *Revelations in Context*, ed. Matthew McBride and James Goldberg (Salt Lake City: The Church of Jesus Christ of Latter-day Saints, 2016).
16. Dallin H. Oaks, "Healing the Sick," *Ensign* or *Liahona*, May 2010, 47, ChurchofJesusChrist.org.
17. Church spokesman Eric Hawkins, quoted in Daniel Woodruff, "The Business behind Christ-Centered Energy Healing," 2KUTV, September 21, 2016, https://kutv.com/news/local/the-business-behind-christ-centered-energy-healing.
18. "The First Presidency Urges Latter-day Saints to Wear Face Masks When Needed and Get Vaccinated against COVID-19," Newsroom, The Church of Jesus Christ of Latter-day Saints, August 12, 2021, https://newsroom.churchofjesuschrist.org/article/first-presidency-message-covid-19-august-2021.
19. *Encyclopedia of Mormonism* (1992), "Miracles," 2:908.
20. James E. Talmage, *Jesus the Christ* (1916), chap. 11 (emphasis added).
21. Stefan Riedel, "Edward Jenner and the History of Smallpox and

Vaccination" *Baylor University Medical Center Proceedings* 18, no. 1 (2005): 21–25, https://doi.org/10.1080/08998280.2005.11928028.

22. For a simple explanation of immunity, see "Immune System," Kids Health, reviewed October 2019, https://kidshealth.org/en/parents/immune.html.
23. See "Vaccine Types," U.S. Department of Health and Human Services, reviewed December 22, 2022, https://www.hhs.gov/immunization/basics/types/index.html; for more on how mRNA vaccines work, see "Understanding COVID-19: How mRNA Vaccines Work," Yale Medicine, February 10, 2021, https://www.yalemedicine.org/news/covid-19-mrna-vaccines.
24. For an overview, see Elaine R. Miller et al., "Deaths Following Vaccination: What Does the Evidence Show?" *Vaccine* 33, no. 29 (2015): 3288–92, https://doi.org/10.1016/j.vaccine.2015.05.023.
25. Paul A. Offit, "The Cutter Incident, 50 Years Later," *New England Journal of Medicine* 352, no. 14 (2005): 1411–12, https://doi.org/10.1056/NEJMp048180; N. Nathanson and A. D. Langmuir, "The Cutter Incident: Poliomyelitis Following Formaldehyde-Inactivated Poliovirus Vaccination in the United States during the Spring of 1955," *American Journal of Epidemiology* 78, no. 1 (1963): 29–60, https://doi.org/10.1093/oxfordjournals.aje.a120328.
26. Paul A. Offit, *The Cutter Incident: How America's First Polio Vaccine Led to the Growing Vaccine Crisis* (New Haven, CT: Yale University Press, 2005).
27. L. B. Schonberger et al., "Guillain-Barré Syndrome Following Vaccination in the National Influenza Immunization Program, United States, 1976–1977," *American Journal of Epidemiology* 110, no. 2 (1979): 105–23, https://doi.org/10.1093/oxfordjournals.aje.a112795.
28. Kurt Link, *The Vaccine Controversy: The History, Use, and Safety of Vaccinations* (Westport, CT: Praeger Publishers, 2005).
29. Miller et al., "Deaths following Vaccination," 3288–92.
30. "The First Presidency and Apostles over Age 70 Receive the COVID-19 Vaccine," Newsroom, The Church of Jesus Christ of Latter day Saints, January 19, 2021, https://newsroom.churchofjesuschrist.org/article/church-leaders-covid-19-vaccine?lang=undefined.
31. "Immunize Children, Leaders Urge," *Liahona,* July 1978, ChurchofJesusChrist.org.
32. "First Presidency and Apostles . . . Receive the COVID-19 Vaccine."
33. "The Family: A Proclamation to the World," ChurchofJesusChrist.org; "Elder Neil L. Andersen: Children Essential to God's Eternal Plan," Church News, October 1, 2011, https://www.thechurchnews.com/2011/10/1/23226320/elder-neil-l-andersen-children-essential-to-gods-eternal-plan.
34. *General Handbook*, 38.6.9.
35. *General Handbook*, 38.6.9.
36. *General Handbook*, 2.1.3.

37. Dallin H. Oaks, "Healing the Sick," *Ensign* or *Liahona*, May 2010, 47, ChurchofJesusChrist.org.
38. "Spinal Muscular Atrophy," MedlinePlus, accessed September 13, 2022, https://medlineplus.gov/genetics/condition/spinal-muscular-atrophy/.
39. Ingrid E. C. Verhaart et al., "Prevalence, Incidence and Carrier Frequency of 5q-Linked Spinal Muscular Atrophy—a Literature Review," *Orphanet Journal of Rare Diseases* 12, no. 1 (2017): 124, https://doi.org/10.1186/s13023-017-0671-8.
40. Stephen F. Kingsmore et al., "Measurement of Genetic Diseases as a Cause of Mortality in Infants Receiving Whole Genome Sequencing," *Nature Portfolio Journal of Genomic Medicine* 5, no. 49 (2020), https://doi.org/10.1038/s41525-020-00155-8.
41. Jocelyn Kaiser, "A Second Chance: A Neuron-Targeting Gene Therapy Delivered into the Blood Saves Infants with a Deadly Spinal Disease—and Boosts an Entire Field," *Science* 358, no. 6363 (2017): 582–85, https://www.science.org/doi/full/10.1126/science.358.6363.582.
42. Bruce R. McConkie, quoted in Robert L. Millet, "Alive in Christ: The Salvation of Little Children," in *The Book of Mormon: Fourth Nephi through Moroni, From Zion to Destruction,* ed. Monte S. Nyman and Charles D. Tate Jr. (1995), 11, available at https://rsc.byu.edu/book/book-mormon-fourth-nephi-through-moroni-zion-destruction.
43. "Mortality," Gospel Topics, topics.ChurchofJesusChrist.org.

Chapter 8: Nature versus Nurture

1. See Gregor J. Mendel, "Versuche über Pflanzen-Hybriden," *Verhandlungen des Naturforschenden Vereines in Brünn*, vol. 4 (1866): 3–47.
2. "Mortality," Gospel Topics, topics.ChurchofJesusChrist.org.
3. D. Todd. Christofferson, "Moral Agency" (devotional address, Brigham Young University, Provo, UT, January 31, 2006), available at https://speeches.byu.edu/talks/d-todd-christofferson/moral-agency/.
4. Scott Freeman et al., *Biological Science*, 6th ed. (Hoboken, NJ: Pearson Higher Education, 2017), 37.
5. Skin color is controlled by a host of different genes working in combination, but the principle is still the same. For a review, see William J. Pavan and Richard A. Sturm, "The Genetics of Human Skin and Hair Pigmentation," *Annual Review of Genomics and Human Genetics* 20 (2019): 41–72, https://doi.org/10.1146/annurev-genom-083118-015230.
6. "Cortisol," Cleveland Clinic, last modified December 10, 2021, https://my.clevelandclinic.org/health/articles/22187-cortisol#:~:text=Regulating%20your%20body's%20stress%20response%3A%20During%20times%20of%20stress%2C%20your,energy%20during%20times%20of%20stress.
7. M. Cutolo et al., "Regulation of Glucocorticoids by the Central Nervous System," *Clinical and Experimental Rheumatology* 29 (2011): 19–22; A. Herane Vives et al., "The Relationship between Cortisol, Stress and Psychiatric Illness: New Insights Using Hair Analysis," *Journal of*

Psychiatric Research 70 (2015): 38–49, https://doi.org/10.1016/j.jpsychires.2015.08.007; S. D. Hewagalamulage et al., "Stress, Cortisol, and Obesity: A Role for Cortisol Responsiveness in Identifying Individuals Prone to Obesity," *Domestic Animal Endocrinology* 56 (2016): S112–20, https://doi.org/10.1016/j.domaniend.2016.03.004.

8. "What Is Epigenetics?," Genomics and Precision Health, Centers for Disease Control and Prevention, accessed September 14, 2022, https://www.cdc.gov/genomics/disease/epigenetics.htm.
9. Benjamin A. Pierce, *Genetics: A Conceptual Approach*, 2nd ed. (W. H. Freeman and Company, 2015).
10. "BRCA Gene Mutations: Cancer Risk and Genetic Testing," National Cancer Institute, last modified November 19, 2020, https://www.cancer.gov/about-cancer/causes-prevention/genetics/brca-fact-sheet.
11. Identical twins are twins that result from one egg and one sperm that split during embryonic development into two babies.
12. Fraternal twins result from two eggs and two sperm; they are the equivalent of siblings being born at the same time.
13. For an overview, see "What Is Heritability," MedlinePlus, last updated September 16, 2023, https://medlineplus.gov/genetics/understanding/inheritance/heritability/.
14. For a detailed review of heritability, see "Heredity and Heritability," *Stanford Encyclopedia of Philosophy*, July 15, 2004, https://stanford.library.sydney.edu.au/archives/spr2008/entries/heredity/.
15. Robert Plomin et al., "Top 10 Replicated Findings from Behavioral Genetics," *Perspectives on Psychological Science* 11, no. 1 (2016): 3–23, https://doi.org/10.1177/1745691615617439.
16. Jeffrey R. Holland, "Like a Broken Vessel," *Ensign* or *Liahona*, November 2013, 40, ChurchofJesusChrist.org.
17. Gitta H. Lubke et al., "Estimating the Genetic Variance of Major Depressive Disorder Due to All Single Nucleotide Polymorphisms," *Biological Psychiatry* 72, no. 8 (2012): 707–9, https://doi.org/10.1016/j.biopsych.2012.03.011.
18. C. M. Middeldorp et al., "The Co-Morbidity of Anxiety and Depression in the Perspective of Genetic Epidemiology: A Review of Twin and Family Studies," *Psychological Medicine* 35, no. 5 (2005): 611–24, https://doi.org/10.1017/s003329170400412x.
19. Stephan Ripke et al., "Genome-Wide Association Analysis Identifies 13 New Risk Loci for Schizophrenia," *Nature Genetics* 45, no. 10 (2013): 1150–59, https://doi.org/10.1038/ng.2742.
20. Trent Gaugler et al., "Most Genetic Risk for Autism Resides with Common Variation," *Nature Genetics* 46, no. 8 (2014): 881–85, https://doi.org/10.1038/ng.3039; Lambertus Klei et al., "Common Genetic Variants, Acting Additively, Are a Major Source of Risk for Autism," *Molecular Autism* 3, no. 9 (2012), https://doi.org/10.1186/2040-2392-3-9.
21. Lea K. Davis et al., "Partitioning the Heritability of Tourette Syndrome and Obsessive Compulsive Disorder Reveals Differences in

Genetic Architecture," *PLoS Genetics* 9, no. 10 (2013), https://doi.org/10.1371/journal.pgen.1003864.

22. For example, G. H. Lubke et al., "Genome-Wide Analyses of Borderline Personality Features," *Molecular Psychiatry* 19, no. 8 (2014): 923–29, https://doi.org/10.1038/mp.2013.109.
23. Plomin et al., "Top 10 Replicated Findings from Behavioral Genetics," 3–23.
24. For example, George F. Koob and Eric P. Zorrilla, "Neurobiological Mechanisms of Addiction: Focus on Corticotropin-Releasing Factor," *Current Opinion in Investigational Drugs* 11, no. 1 (2010): 63 [PMID: 20047160].
25. Peter J. Hamilton and Eric J. Nestler, "Epigenetics and Addiction," *Current Opinions in Neurobiology* 59 (2019): 128–36, https://doi.org/10.1016/j.conb.2019.05.005.
26. Shao-Cheng Wang et al., "Opioid Addiction, Genetic Susceptibility, and Medical Treatments: A Review," *International Journal of Molecular Sciences* 20, no. 17 (2019): 4294, https://doi.org/10.3390/ijms20174294; Dana B. Hancock et al., "Human Genetics of Addiction: New Insights and Future Directions," *Current Psychiatry Reports* 20, no. 8 (2018), https://doi.org/10.1007/s11920-018-0873-3.
27. Marina R. Picciotto and Paul J. Kenny, "Mechanisms of Nicotine Addiction," *Cold Spring Harbor Perspectives in Medicine* 11, no. 5 (2021): a039610, https://doi.org/10.1101/cshperspect.a039610.
28. Holly R. Thomasson et al., "Low Frequency of the ADH2*2 Allele among Atayal Natives of Taiwan with Alcohol Use Disorders," *Alcohol: Clinical and Experimental Research* 18, no. 3 (1994): 640–43, https://doi.org/10.1111/j.1530-0277.1994.tb00923.x.
29. Tamiko Konishi et al., "The ADH3*2 and CYP2E1 c2 Alleles Increase the Risk of Alcoholism in Mexican American Men," *Experimental and Molecular Pathology* 74, no. 2 (2003): 183–89, https://doi.org/10.1016/s0014-4800(03)00006-6; Fang Sun et al., "Contribution of Genetic Polymorphisms in Ethanol-Metabolizing Enzymes to Problem Drinking Behavior in Middle-Aged Japanese Men," *Behavior Genetics* 32, no. 4 (2002): 229–36, https://doi.org/10.1023/a:1019711812074.
30. Gabor Oroszi and David Goldman, "Alcoholism: Genes and Mechanisms," *Pharmacogenomics* 5, no. 8 (2004): 1037–48, https://doi.org/10.1517/14622416.5.8.1037.
31. Todd Love et al., "Neuroscience of Internet Pornography Addiction: A Review and Update," *Behavior Science (Basel)* 5, no. 3 (2015): 388–433, https://www.ncbi.nlm.nih.gov/pmc/articles/PMC4600144/.
32. "New Church Website on Same-Sex Attraction Offers Love, Understanding, and Hope," Newsroom, The Church of Jesus Christ of Latter-day Saints, December 6, 2012, https://newsroom.churchofjesuschrist.org/article/church-website-same-sex-attraction.
33. Daniel A. Warner, "Sex Determination in Reptiles," *Hormones and Reproduction of Vertebrates* (2011): 1–38, https://doi.org/10.1016

/B978-0-12-374930-7.10001-9; for a review of sex determination in animals, see Doris Bachtrog et al., "Sex Determination: Why So Many Ways of Doing It?," *PLoS Biology*, July 1, 2014, https://journals.plos.org/plosbiology/article?id=10.1371/journal.pbio.1001899.

34. Jeannie Visootsak and John M. Graham Jr., "Klinefelter Syndrome and Other Sex Chromosomal Aneuploidies," *Orphanet Journal of Rare Diseases* 1, no. 42 (2006), https://doi.org/10.1186/1750-1172-1-42.
35. See Arthur C. Guyton and John E. Hall, *Guyton and Hall Textbook of Medical Physiology*, 13th ed. (Philadelphia: Elsevier, 2016).
36. Richard E. Jones and Kristin H. Lopez, "Puberty," chap. 6, in *Human Reproductive Biology*, 4th ed. (London: Academic Press, 2014), 103–18, https://doi.org/10.1016/B978-0-12-382184-3.00006-4.
37. David Skuse et al., "Sex Chromosome Aneuploidies," *Handbook of Clinical Neurology* 147 (2018): 355–76, https://doi.org/10.1016/B978-0-444-63233-3.00024-5.
38. Agnethe Berglund et al., "The Epidemiology of Sex Chromosome Abnormalities," *American Journal of Medical Genetics Part C: Seminars in Medical Genetics* 184, no. 2 (2020): 202–15, https://doi.org/10.1002/ajmg.c.31805.
39. "SRY Gene," MedlinePlus, accessed September 14, 2022, https://medlineplus.gov/genetics/gene/sry/#:~:text=The%20SRY%20gene%20provides%20instructions,46%20chromosomes%20in%20each%20cell.
40. For additional information, see "Androgen Insensitivity Syndrome," MedlinePlus, accessed February 18, 2023, https://medlineplus.gov/genetics/condition/androgen-insensitivity-syndrome/#frequency.
41. We are intentionally limiting the acronym to LGBT+ because the majority of the research has not branched beyond these four groups.
42. Melinda C. Mills, "Genetic Loci Linked with Same-Sex Sexual Behavior Cannot Predict Orientation of Individuals," *Science* 365, no. 6456 (2019): 869–70, https://doi.org/10.1126/science.aay2726.
43. Niklas Långström et al., "Genetic and Environmental Effects on Same-Sex Sexual Behavior: A Population Study of Twins in Sweden," *Archives of Sexual Behavior* 39, no. 1 (2010): 75–80, https://doi.org/10.1007/s10508-008-9386-1.
44. Andrea Ganna et al., "Large-Scale GWAS Reveals Insights into the Genetic Architecture of Same-Sex Sexual Behavior," *Science* 365, no. 6456 (2019), https://doi.org/10.1126/science.aat7693; According to the authors, "The range reflects differing estimates by using different analysis methods or prevalence assumptions."
45. Ganna et al., "Large-Scale GWAS Reveals Insights"; Mills, "How Do Genes Affect Same-Sex Behavior?," 869–70.
46. M. E. Goddard et al., "Genetics of Complex Traits: Prediction of Phenotype, Identification of Causal Polymorphisms and Genetic Architecture," *Proceedings of the Royal Society B: Biological Sciences* (2016), https://doi.org/10.1098/rspb.2016.0569.
47. For example, *Encyclopaedia Britannica*, s.v. "Gender Identity," modified February 15, 2023, https://www.britannica.com/topic/gender

-identity; Veronica Zambon, "What Are Some Different Types of Gender Identity?" *Medical News Today*, updated January 3, 2023, https://www.medicalnewstoday.com/articles/types-of-gender-identity.

48. "About 47, XXY (Klinefelter Syndrome)," The Association for X and Y Chromosome Variations, accessed October 24, 2022, https://genetic.org/variations/about-47xxy/; Cynthia M. Smith and William J. Bremner, "Klinefelter Syndrome," *Archives of Internal Medicine* 158, no. 12 (1998): 1309–14; "What Are Common Symptoms of Klinefelter Syndrome (KS)," National Institutes of Health, accessed October 26, 2022, https://www.nichd.nih.gov/health/topics/klinefelter/condition info/symptoms.
49. See, for a detailed discussion, James M. Cantor, "Transgender and Gender Diverse Children and Adolescents: Fact-Checking of AAP Policy," *Journal of Sex & Marital Therapy* 46, no. 4 (2019): 307–13, https://doi.org/10.1080/0092623X.2019.1698481.
50. For example, Annika Johansson et al., "A Five-Year Follow-Up Study of Swedish Adults with Gender Identity Disorder," *Archives of Sexual Behavior* 39, no. 6 (2010): 1429–37; Griet de Cuypere, "Sexual and Physical Health after Sex Reassignment Surgery," *Archives of Sexual Behavior* 34, no. 6 (2005): 679–90; Louis J. Gooren et al., "Long-Term Treatment of Transsexuals with Cross-Sex Hormones," *The Journal of Clinical Endocrinology and Metabolism* 93, no. 1 (2008): 19–25; Cecilia Dhejne et al., "Long-Term Follow-Up of Transsexual Persons Undergoing Sex Reassignment Surgery: Cohort Study in Sweden," *PLoS One* 6, no. 2 (2011): e16885, https://doi.org/10.1371/journal.pone.0016885.
51. Stephen B. Levine et al., "Reconsidering Informed Consent for Trans-Identified Children, Adolescents, and Young Adults," *Journal of Sex & Marital Therapy* 48, no. 7 (2022): 706–27, https://doi.org/10.1080/0092623X.2022.2046221; E. Coleman et al., "Standards of Care for the Health of Transgender and Gender Diverse People," *International Journal of Transgender Health* 23, no.1 (2022): S1-S259.
52. Dallin H. Oaks, in "Trib Talk: LDS Leaders Oaks, Christofferson Will Appear on Trib Talk to Discuss Religious Freedom . . ." (video), *Salt Lake Tribune*, January 29, 2015, available on YouTube, https://www.youtube.com/watch?v=UIJ6gL_xc-M.
53. "The Family: A Proclamation to the World," ChurchofJesusChrist .org.
54. "General Conference Leadership Meetings Begin," Newsroom, The Church of Jesus Christ of Latter-day Saints, accessed September 18, 2022, https://newsroom.churchofjesuschrist.org/article /october-2019-general-conference-first-presidency-leadership-session ?cid=HP_NWSRM_10_2_19.
55. Russell M. Nelson, in "Worldwide Devotional for Young Adults with President Nelson—May 2022," broadcasts.ChurchofJesusChrist.org.
56. D. Todd Christofferson, "The Purpose of This Website," Same-Sex Attraction, The Church of Jesus Christ of Latter-day Saints, https://

www.churchofjesuschrist.org/topics/gay/videos/purpose-of-this-website?lang=eng.

57. David A. Bednar. "Things as They Really Are," *Ensign*, June 2010, 16, ChurchofJesusChrist.org.
58. Thomas S. Monson, "The Will Within," *Ensign*, May 1987, 67, ChurchofJesusChrist.org.
59. Christofferson, "Moral Agency."
60. "History, 1838–1856, volume C-1 [2 November 1838–31 July 1842]," 1253, The Joseph Smith Papers, accessed November 25, 2022, https://www.josephsmithpapers.org/paper-summary/history-1838-1856-volume-c-1-2-november-1838-31-july-1842/425.

Chapter 9: Environmental Stewardship

1. See, for example, "Creation Care," Christianity Today, accessed September 14, 2022, https://www.christianitytoday.com/ct/topics/c/creation-care/; "Why Should Christians Care for Creation?" BioLogos, last updated August 8, 2022, https://biologos.org/common-questions/why-should-christians-care-for-creation; "Creation Care FAQs," Evangelical Environmental Network, accessed September 14, 2022, https://creationcare.org/who-we-are/beliefs.html.
2. Russell M. Nelson, "The Creation," *Ensign*, May 2000, 84, ChurchofJesusChrist.org.
3. Ellen F. Davis, "The Meaning of Dominion," Bible Odyssey, accessed February 15, 2023, https://www.bibleodyssey.org/passages/related-articles/the-meaning-of-dominion/.
4. These data are not yet published.
5. Marcus B. Nash, "Righteous Dominion and Compassion for the Earth," Newsroom, The Church of Jesus Christ of Latter-day Saints, April 12, 2013, https://newsroom.churchofjesuschrist.org/article/elder-nash-stegner-symposium.
6. Neal A. Maxwell, *A Wonderful Flood of Light* (Salt Lake City: Bookcraft, 1990), 103.
7. Gérald Caussé, "Our Earthly Stewardship" (general conference address, October 2022), ChurchofJesusChrist.org.
8. "Major Gaps between the Public, Scientists on Key Issues," Pew Research Center, July 1, 2015, https://www.pewresearch.org/internet/interactives/public-scientists-opinion-gap/.
9. Rebecca Lindsey, "How Do We Know the Build-Up of Carbon Dioxide in the Atmosphere Is Caused by Humans?" Climate.gov, October 12, 2022, https://www.climate.gov/news-features/climate-qa/how-do-we-know-build-carbon-dioxide-atmosphere-caused-humans.
10. "Global Time Series," National Centers for Environmental Information, accessed September 14, 2022, https://www.ncei.noaa.gov/access/monitoring/climate-at-a-glance/global/time-series.
11. Ice traps small particles of atmosphere containing chemical isotopes that can tell us a range of potential temperatures of the air when it was trapped; for more information, see Bethan Davies, "Ice Core Basics,

AntarcticGlaciers.org, last updated June 22, 2020, https://www.antarcticglaciers.org/glaciers-and-climate/ice-cores/ice-core-basics/.

12. Tree growth is highly dependent on ambient temperatures (and the affected moisture levels), so scientists can determine temperature by looking at the size of tree rings; for more information, see Bruce Bauer, "How Tree Rings Tell Time and Climate History," Climate.gov, November 29, 2018, https://www.climate.gov/news-features/blogs/beyond-data/how-tree-rings-tell-time-and-climate-history.
13. Pollen trapped in fossilized sediments can tell us what types of plants were alive at the time of deposit; this then indicates potential climate ranges; see "Pollen: More Than Just an Allergen," Center for Science Education, University Corporation for Atmospheric Research, https://scied.ucar.edu/learning-zone/how-climate-works/pollen-more-just-allergen.
14. Coral and cave stalagmites both trap oxygen isotopes, which can indicate temperatures at the time they formed; for more information, see "How Can Corals Teach Us about Climate?" National Centers for Environmental Information, June 8, 2016, https://www.ncei.noaa.gov/news/how-can-corals-teach-us-about-climate.
15. "Climate Time Machine," NASA, accessed October 27, 2022, https://climate.nasa.gov/interactives/climate-time-machine.
16. Michon Scott and Rebecca Lindsey, "What's the Hottest Earth's Ever Been?," Climate.gov, June 18, 2020, https://www.climate.gov/news-features/climate-qa/whats-hottest-earths-ever-been.
17. Thomas Knutson et al., "Tropical Cyclones and Climate Change," *Nature Geoscience* 3, no. 3 (2010): 157–63, https://doi.org/10.1038/ngeo779.
18. Sandra McCubbin et al., "Where Does Climate Fit? Vulnerability to Climate Change in the Context of Multiple Stressors in Funafuti, Tuvalu," *Global Environmental Change* 30 (2015): 43–55, https://doi.org/10.1016/j.gloenvcha.2014.10.007.
19. Frederick M. Burkle Jr. et al., "The Changing Face of Humanitarian Crises," *Brown Journal of World Affairs* 20, no. 2 (2014): 19–36, https://bjwa.brown.edu/20-2/the-changing-face-of-humanitarian-crises/.
20. Xiaoxu Wu et al., "Impact of Climate Change on Human Infectious Diseases," *Environment International* 86 (2016): 14–23, https://doi.org/10.1016/j.envint.2015.09.007.
21. Scott C. Doney et al., "Ocean Acidification: The Other CO2 Problem," *Annual Review of Marine Science* 1 (2009): 169–92, https://doi.org/10.1146/annurev.marine.010908.163834.
22. Oystein Wiig, Jon Aars, and Erik W. Born, "Effects of Climate Change on Polar Bears," *Science Progress* 91, no. 2 (2008): 151–73, https://doi.org/10.3184/003685008X324506.
23. Rui Rosa et al., "Biological Responses of Sharks to Ocean Acidification," *Biology Letters* 13 (2017), https://doi.org/10.1098/rsbl.2016.0796.
24. Alan Buis, "Steamy Relationships: How Atmospheric Water Vapor Amplifies Earth's Greenhouse Effect," Ask NASA Climate, February

8, 2022, https://climate.nasa.gov/ask-nasa-climate/3143/steamy-relationships-how-atmospheric-water-vapor-amplifies-earths-greenhouse-effect/.

25. For more information, see "What Is the Greenhouse Effect?," ACS, https://www.acs.org/content/acs/en/climatescience/climatesciencenarratives/what-is-the-greenhouse-effect.html.
26. Buis, "Steamy Relationships: How Atmospheric Water Vapor Amplifies Earth's Greenhouse Effect."
27. Alan Buis, "The Atmosphere: Getting a Handle on Carbon Dioxide," NASA Global Climate Change, October 9, 2019, https://climate.nasa.gov/news/2915/the-atmosphere-getting-a-handle-on-carbon-dioxide/.
28. "Why Does CO2 Get Most of the Attention When There Are So Many Other Heat-Trapping Gases?" Union of Concerned Scientists, last updated August 3, 2017, https://www.ucsusa.org/resources/why-does-co2-get-more-attention-other-gases.
29. "Observation Package (ObsPack) Data Products," Global Monitoring Laboratory, Earth System Research Laboratories, National Oceanic and Atmospheric Administration, accessed September 14, 2022, https://gml.noaa.gov/ccgg/obspack.
30. Scientists can use ice cores with trapped bubbles of atmosphere to estimate atmospheric CO2 levels from the past.
31. "Trends in Atmospheric Carbon Dioxide," Global Monitoring Laboratory, accessed September 14, 2022, https://gml.noaa.gov/ccgg/trends/history.html.
32. See "The Technical Details: Chemistry Composition of an Atom," Global Monitoring Laboratory, https://gml.noaa.gov/ccgg/isotopes/chemistry.html.
33. For more information, see "The Basics: Stable Carbon and the Carbon Cycle," Global Monitoring Laboratory, https://gml.noaa.gov/ccgg/isotopes/stable.html.
34. See "The Basics: 14C and Fossil Fuels," Global Monitoring Laboratory, https://gml.noaa.gov/ccgg/isotopes/c14tracer.html.
35. Lindsey, "How Do We Know the Build-Up of Carbon Dioxide in the Atmosphere Is Caused by Humans?"; Matthew R. Heal, "The Application of Carbon-14 Analyses to the Source Apportionment of Atmospheric Carbonaceous Particulate Matter: A Review," *Analytical & Bioanalytical Chemistry* 406, no. 1 (2013): 81–98.
36. David Jablonski and W. G. Chaloner, "Extinctions in the Fossil Record [and Discussion]," *Philosophical Transactions: Biological Sciences* 344, no. 1307 (1994): 11–17, https://www.jstor.org/stable/56148.
37. Anthony D. Barnosky et al., "Has the Earth's Sixth Mass Extinction Already Arrived?" *Nature* 471 (2011): 51–57, https://doi.org/10.1038/nature09678.
38. Barnosky et al., "Earth's Sixth Mass Extinction," 51–57.
39. "Summary Statistics," International Union for Conservation of

Nature's Red List, accessed September 14, 2022, https://www.iucnredlist.org/resources/summary-statistics.

40. David L. Wagner, "Insect Declines in the Anthropocene," *Annual Review of Entomology* 65 (2020): 457–80, https://doi.org/10.1146/annurev-ento-011019-025151.
41. Gina Darnaud, "Shrinking Bee Populations Are Being Replaced by Human Pollinators," Global Citizen, April 19, 2016, https://www.globalcitizen.org/en/content/life-without-bees-hand-human-pollination-rural-chi/.
42. John W. Day Jr. et al., "Restoration of the Mississippi Delta: Lessons from Hurricanes Katrina and Rita," *Science* 315, no. 5819 (2007): 1679–84, https://www.science.org/doi/10.1126/science.1137030.
43. For example, Anne M. Rowzee et al., "Glucagon-Like Peptide-1 Gene Therapy," *Journal of Diabetes Research* (2011), https://doi.org/10.1155/2011/601047.
44. Hiroshi Tamura et al., "Outstanding Contributions of LAL Technology to Pharmaceutical and Medical Science," *Biomedicines* 9, no. 5 (2021): 536, https://doi.org/10.3390/biomedicines9050536.
45. Kalila Morsink, "With Every Breath You Take, Thank the Ocean," Ocean, Smithsonian, accessed October 25, 2022, https://ocean.si.edu/ocean-life/plankton/every-breath-you-take-thank-ocean.
46. Bingmiao Gao et al., "Cone Snails: A Big Store of Conotoxins for Novel Drug Discovery," *Toxins* 9, no. 12 (2017): 397, https://doi.org/10.3390/toxins9120397.
47. Nash, "Righteous Dominion and Compassion for the Earth."
48. Joseph Fielding Smith, *Doctrines of Salvation: Sermons and Writings of Joseph Fielding Smith,* 3 vols., ed. Bruce R. McConkie (Salt Lake City: Bookcraft, 1960), 1:84.
49. Garrett Hardin, "The Tragedy of the Commons," *Science* 162, no. 3859 (1968): 1243–48, https://doi.org/10.1126/science.162.3859.1243.
50. L. Tom Perry, "Train Up a Child," *Ensign*, November 1988, 73, ChurchofJesusChrist.org.
51. See Loren C. Eiseley, "The Star Thrower," in *The Unexpected Universe* (New York: Harcourt, Brace, and World, 1969), 69–72.
52. Nash, "Righteous Dominion and Compassion for the Earth."

Conclusion

1. "Why Do Leaves Change Color in the Fall?," Smithsonian, accessed September 18, 2022, https://www.si.edu/stories/why-do-leaves-change-color-fall.

INDEX